Heavenly Handmade
BAGS

OVER 25 DESIGNS TO STITCH, KNIT, EMBROIDER & EMBELLISH

Sue Hawkins

David and Charles

For Cherry and Annie – my very good friends and fellow old bags

A DAVID & CHARLES BOOK
Copyright © David & Charles Limited 2006

David & Charles is an F+W Publications Inc. company
4700 East Galbraith Road
Cincinnati, OH 45236

First published in the UK in 2006

Text and designs copyright © Sue Hawkins 2006

ISBN-13: 978-0-7153-2142-3 hardback
ISBN-10: 0-7153-2142-0 hardback

ISBN-13: 978-0-7153-2143-0 paperback (USA only)
ISBN-10: 0-7153-2143-9 paperback (USA only)

Printed in China by R R Donnelley
for David & Charles
Brunel House   Newton Abbot   Devon

Commissioning Editor   Vivienne Wells
Project Editor   Lin Clements
Editor   Ame Verso
Executive Art Editor   Ali Myer
Designer   Charly Bailey
Production Controller   Ros Napper

Visit our website at www.davidandcharles.co.uk

David & Charles books are available from all good bookshops; alternatively you
can contact our Orderline on 0870 9908222 or write to us at FREEPOST EX2 110,
D&C Direct, Newton Abbot, TQ12 4ZZ (no stamp required UK only); US customers
call 800-289-0963 and Canadian customers call 800-840-5220.

Contents

Introduction

In this book there are 27 bags to make; mostly small and richly stitched, with the addition of gleaming beads, jewels and pretty feathers. These little bags do not hold the necessities of daily life; they are exotic flights of fancy that will carry your dreams, and maybe a lipstick!

My real love is embroidery of all descriptions but really anything created with a needle and thread takes my fancy. I am also passionate about the making up and finishing of lovely pieces of work. So the opportunity to make tiny pieces of whatever type of embroidery I liked and turn them into little bags was perfect – so here is my collection of heavenly bags.

Knitting isn't really my craft but I couldn't resist introducing some into this collection so please excuse me if the knitting pattern is in my own style. I haven't used abbreviations and so the patterns don't look like algebra, but I hope mine will be easier to follow for somebody who only knows knitting basics.

I haven't listed any thread alternatives for any of the embroidered projects because I took a great deal of trouble choosing the colours and threads and love the way that they work with each other. If you change to the nearest available in another range the colours won't work with each other in quite the same way. I think that however carefully a substitution has been done, you will never get quite as good an effect using a different set of threads to those I stitched with and you might end up disappointed. If you want to change to another make of thread then choose a set of colours that look well together in their own right. Refer to Suppliers on page 118 for the threads and materials I used. Unless otherwise stated in the chart keys, one skein of each colour of cotton (floss) or tapestry wool (yarn) has been used.

The projects employ many interesting counted stitches in lovely colour combinations. Although many are worked on canvas, this is definitely not tapestry with acres of boring tent stitch. In fact, there is hardly a tent stitch in sight and certainly no beige backgrounds. All the stitches used are described and illustrated on pages 108–113. The designs are created from the infinite effects and patterns produced by combining these stitch shapes and rich colours. I would like you to take my ideas and make them your own by adding trimmings and choosing different colour ranges. Have fun when you go shopping and allow yourself to buy pieces of fabric just because you like them. It is amazing how ideas flow when you have a pile of lovely cloth in front of you.

The bags make lovely gifts for mothers and grandmothers to give to daughters and granddaughters, or for special friends to give to each other – and what better present to give or receive than a bag you made yourself?

Easiest Bag in the World

This is the easiest way of making a bag that I know: simply sew three pieces of fabric together, fold in half, sew down the sides, turn right side out, stitch up the lining and push it down inside! You could make one to match your outfit in half an hour before you go out this evening, especially if, like me, you have some lovely fabrics to hand. I am absolutely unrepentant about the amount of fabric pieces I have. I collect silky bits and shiny bobs without the slightest idea of what I might do with them. One of these pieces, with a few trimmings, can be transformed into a present in no time at all and everybody likes to receive something handmade. I have made three small bags here but the method works for larger sizes too – for work bags, shoe bags and shopping bags.

Finished bag size, excluding handles: 22 x 20cm (8 x 8½in)

1 Lay the oblong piece for the bag right side up on your table. Pin a handle to each end, laying the handles over the bag fabric and lining up the ends with the edges of the fabric.

2 Lay a piece of lining right side down over each end of the bag and sew the seam of the lining to the bag. These seams will be the top edge of the finished bag and as you sew them you will be attaching the handles as well. In the picture below you can see the red brocade bag before it was stitched up the sides. Sew any bands of braid or trimmings on at this stage.

3 You will now have a long strip with lining at one end, a handle, then the bag fabric, another handle and the other piece of lining. Fold the whole lot across the middle of the bag piece right sides together and matching up the side seams. Now sew the side seams and lining pieces to produce a long, deep shape. Turn right sides out.

4 Turn the edges of the bottom of the lining in and topstitch across the seam. Push the lining down inside the bag to finish.

Tip If you are using ribbon for the handles, sew two pieces wrong sides together to give you double-sided handles and make them a little stiffer.

This partly made bag (shown completed opposite) reveals how simple the construction is.

The Easiest Bag in the World can have many different looks, as seen by the variations in this chapter. The bag on page 7 uses pink and purple fabrics patched together in squares, with a glamorous maribou feather trim to the seams below the handles. The striped silk bag (far right) can be made very quickly at little cost. It uses antique gold braid as a diagonal trim and for the handles too, and is embellished with deep mauve maribou feather. The red brocade bag (right) is another lovely little evening bag. The fabric has an Indian look, teamed with handles of orange velvet with a metallic gold edge.

Teddy Bear Bag

This little bag with its plump teddy bear started as a gift for a child but it has become one of my favourites and I shall certainly use it myself. The teddy is worked in velvet stitch to give him a fluffy look and make him stand out from the tent stitch rug he is sitting on. Long-legged cross stitch finishes off the rug. Velvet stitch is cross stitch but with an extra long looped stitch in between the two crosses; it's simple enough to do but a bit more time consuming. If you are in a hurry you could work the whole bear in cross stitch – he will be nearly as good but I do think the effort with the velvet stitch is well worth it. You can cut the loops of velvet stitch once it has been worked to make a soft pile effect a bit like carpet, but I decided that I liked the rougher effect of the loops.

Finished bag size, excluding handles: 15 x 15cm (6 x 6in)

Tip Velvet stitch (see page 113) has to be worked in rows from bottom to top and left to right, so you cannot work areas of one colour as you usually would for cross stitch. Leave threads hanging to work the stripes of colour that run up his body and pick them up on each row.

1 Prepare the canvas for work (see page 106) and follow the chart opposite. Some of the squares on the chart show the same colour but have a different symbol: those with a dot are worked in cross stitch and those with a line are worked in velvet stitch.

2 Work the cross stitch areas first using six strands of stranded cotton, starting in the centre with the bear's bow in two reds and then counting carefully to the paw pads and soles of the feet.

3 Now work the bear's nose, mouth, eyes and inside his ears in cross stitch, some in two strands of crewel wool and some in six strands of stranded cotton, as indicated by the chart key.

4 Begin working the rows of velvet stitch using two strands of crewel wool, starting at the bottom of the foot on the left of the chart (the bear's right foot). As you make the loop of each stitch catch it with your needle and pull it to make all the loops about the same length. Work up that foot until you start to work rows right across the lower body and on to the other leg and foot. Gradually work up the body and on to the head, working round the cross stitch areas and always working rows from left to right (see Tip).

5 Work the background carpet pattern in tent stitch using four strands of crewel wool. Finish with a row of long-legged cross stitch (see page 110) all around the embroidered square using four strands of navy crewel wool.

Making up

1 Stretch the canvas piece to bring it back to square (see page 106). However carefully you have stitched, it will still have distorted a little and the stretching process will restore the shape and also even up your tension a little. Trim the bare canvas edges to 1.25cm (½in).

2 Use 85cm (33in) lengths of crewel wool to make the tassels. Take two threads of each of the rug colours, fold in half and in half again. Take a further length of navy, fold it double, twist it tightly and loop it around the mid point of the tassel strands, so that the tassel lies in the loop and then allow it to twist to make a cord for the tassel. Thread another double thread of navy in your needle, fold the tassel at the cord and wind it tightly around 1cm (⅜in) from the top. Finish off securely by stitching through the windings and leaving an end hanging amongst the tassel threads. Trim the ends of the tassel to about 5cm (2in) long. Make a second tassel in the same way.

3 Using the finished embroidery as a pattern, cut a piece of backing fabric and two pieces of lining.

4 Pin the tassels to the bottom of the embroidery and then place the backing and embroidery right sides together and sew the sides and bottom edge together attaching the tassels as you do this. Take care to get your stitches very close to the edge of the long-legged cross stitch. Remove pins, turn right side out and the row of long-legged cross stitch should look like a braid around the edge of the bag. Pin the ends of the cord to either side of the bag adjusting the length to suit.

5 Sew the side seams of the lining. Place the lining over the bag wrong side out and sew the top seam of the lining to the bag around the top edge. Pull the lining up from the bag. Turn the edges of the bottom in, topstitch them together and then push the lining down inside the bag to finish.

A tassel made from the wool colours used in the bag embroidery makes a lovely finishing touch.

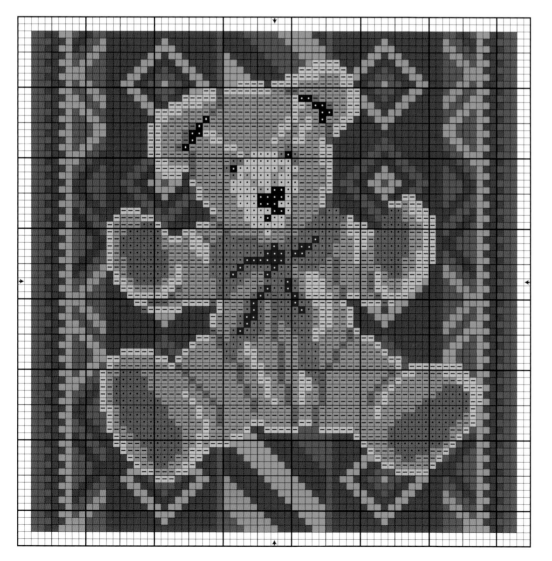

KEY Teddy Bear Bag

DMC stranded cotton

◾	355	cross stitch
◼	814	cross stitch
◾	839	cross stitch
◼	3031	cross stitch

Appletons crewel wool

◼	405	tent stitch
▨	695	tent stitch
▧	721	tent stitch
◼	725	tent stitch (2 skeins)
◼	749	tent stitch (2 skeins)
◾	904	cross stitch
◾	903	cross stitch
▫	901	cross stitch
▬	904	velvet stitch
▬	903	velvet stitch
▭	901	velvet stitch

Turkish Tassels

I love old ethnic textiles, especially highly embroidered ones. The patterns on this useful bag were inspired by a rug I found while travelling in Greece and the box-shape is based on a horse's nose bag, which I have hanging in my sitting room. The nose bag is an old Banjara gypsy piece that is covered in richly coloured embroidery complete with tassels hanging on the bottom. These Indian Gypsies roamed the country finding time to embellish all sorts of everyday textiles with rich embroidery. I am always amazed at the amount of work that was put into such ordinary and utilitarian items. One can only wonder whether the horse really appreciated all that beautiful stitching as he munched his way through his supper.

Finished bag size, excluding handles: 17.5 x 13.5cm (6¾ x 5¼in)

1 Prepare the pieces of canvas for working (see page 106) and then follow the charts overleaf. See page 108 for working the stitches. All the colours are muted by using a mixture of two shades together in the needle – see the chart key for details. The opposite sides of the bag are the same so work the largest pieces of the charts twice, working all four sides using three strands of crewel wool and tent stitch. Try to use diagonal tent stitch for filling shapes once outlines have been worked, as this will distort the canvas less and make stretching easier. Note: the side charts have been rotated to fit the page.

2 Work the base square, then four of the small shapes for the tassels. Each of these is made of two squares two canvas threads apart.

3 Work the handle strap: mine is 62cm (24½in) long but you can lengthen or shorten it by working less or more. The chart shows one pattern repeat, simply keep going back to the beginning until yours is the right length.

Making up

1 Stretch all the canvas pieces to bring them back to square (see page 106). However carefully you have stitched it will still have distorted a little and the stretching process will restore the shape and even up your tension. Trim the bare canvas edges to 1.25cm (½in) on all the large pieces.

2 Take the five bag pieces and the handle and use these as patterns to cut out six pieces of cotton lining.

3 Use 85cm (33in) lengths of yarn to make the four tassels. Take two threads of each pink and cut these four threads in half. Take one of these sets and twist them until they double back to make a cord. Fold in half, knot to make a short length of cord and set this aside. Take one thread of each colour, fold in half and in half again. Take the other set of pink threads and twist as before but before you fold in half to make the cord, loop it around the mid point of the tassel strands so the tassel lies in the loop and then allow it to twist to make a cord. Now take one thread of each pink and thread all four ends in your needle leaving a loop at the bottom. Fold the tassel at the cord and make a loop around it by laying the doubled threads around the neck of the tassel 1cm (⅜in) from the top and then passing the needle through the loop at the end of the thread. Wind tightly around a few times and finish off by stitching through the windings, leaving an end hanging amongst the tassel threads. Trim the tassel ends to 4cm (1½in). Repeat three times to make four sets of cords and tassels.

Tip You could very easily add a zipped pocket to the inside of this bag to keep valuables safe – see page 107 for further instructions on making pockets.

4 Take the four small pieces of embroidery for the tassels. Trim the canvas to within 1cm (⅜in) of the edge of the embroidery and clip the corners. Fold in all the canvas edges leaving one thread of canvas exposed. To make the humbug shape, fold the oblong in half along the empty canvas threads. Work long-legged cross stitch (see page 110) in pinks down these empty threads. When you reach the corner, carry on with the long-legged cross stitch, making a seam by taking one canvas thread from each folded-over edge. As you do this, tuck in one end of the tassel cord halfway along. Now continue up the third side and finish off at the top. Fold the open top edge in the opposite way to make a humbug shape – you will be bringing the ends of the two rows of long-legged cross stitch together at the middle of the next seam. As you join this final seam tuck in the cord, and before you complete the seam, stuff the shape with a tight filling of polyester stuffing (or cotton wool or left-over threads). Repeat for the other three tassels.

5 On all the larger bag pieces fold in all the canvas edges leaving one thread of canvas exposed. When stitching the long-legged cross stitch use two threads of light pink and one of dark pink together in the needle. Take two side pieces and put the wrong sides together. Line up the seam down one long edge and work long-legged cross stitch, taking one canvas thread from each folded-over edge. Take great care to line up exactly and when you reach the end of the seam you should find that the canvas threads match on both sides. Join all four side seams in this way.

The three-dimensional tassels on this bag are a little unusual. The shape is actually a tetrahedron but I call them humbugs because they look like those old-fashioned boiled sweets.

6 Join the bottom of the bag in the same way, tucking the cord from a tassel in at each corner as you stitch.

7 Work long-legged cross stitch along each side of the handle embroidery. Trim the bare canvas edges to 1.25cm (½in). The long-legged cross stitch will naturally fold the edges in. Take the handle lining piece, fold the edges in to fit the handle and slipstitch to the back of the handle. Now work a row of long-legged cross stitch all around the top of the bag attaching the handle with a long-legged seam to the top of two opposite sides as you go. Turn down the top edge.

8 Take the five lining pieces and stitch them together down the sides and then add the bottom. Push the lining into the bag and slipstitch it neatly in place around the top to finish the bag.

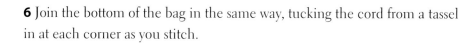

Side – work 2

Side – work 2

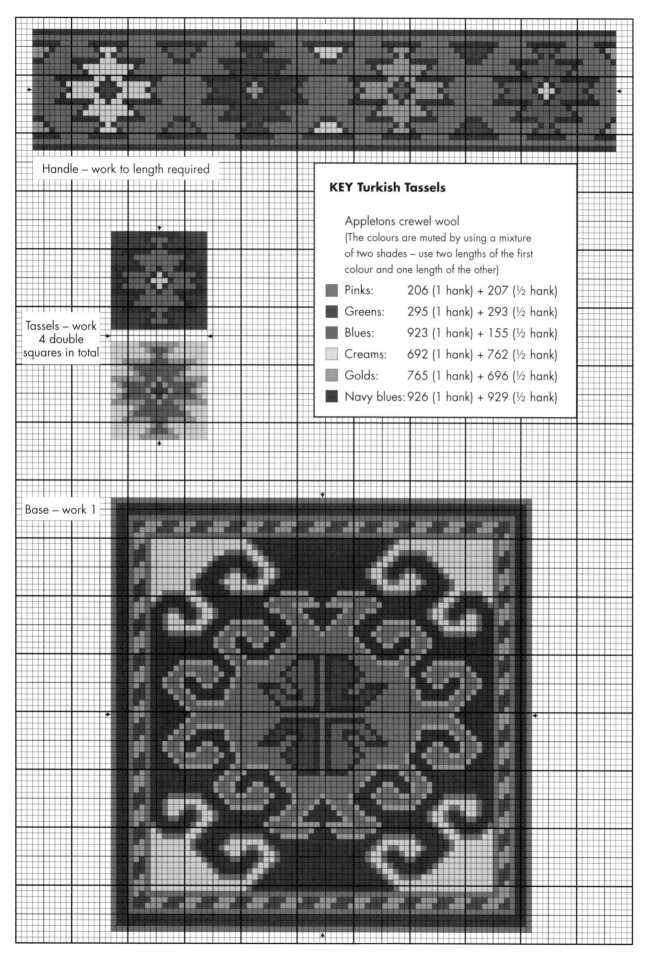

Handle – work to length required

Tassels – work
4 double
squares in total

Base – work 1

KEY Turkish Tassels

Appletons crewel wool
(The colours are muted by using a mixture
of two shades – use two lengths of the first
colour and one length of the other)

Pinks:	206 (1 hank)	+ 207 (½ hank)
Greens:	295 (1 hank)	+ 293 (½ hank)
Blues:	923 (1 hank)	+ 155 (½ hank)
Creams:	692 (1 hank)	+ 762 (½ hank)
Golds:	765 (1 hank)	+ 696 (½ hank)
Navy blues:	926 (1 hank)	+ 929 (½ hank)

Clarice Cliff Satchel

Clarice Cliff was one of the best known designers of ceramics from the English Staffordshire Potteries in the 1930s. Her style was distinctive and unique, the shapes she used were angular, the colours extremely bright and the designs were known collectively as 'Bizarre' ware. The design I have adapted for my bag is based on her Blue W design which was one of the most popular. The embroidered panel is worked in tent stitch and diagonal tent stitch and I used a bright moiré satin to make up the bag because the way the moiré catches the light enhances the vivid design. I then found the plastic buttons in such good colours that I had to add them; they don't have a function but seem to finish off the bag beautifully.

Finished bag size, excluding handles: 25.5 x 21.5cm (10 x 8½in)

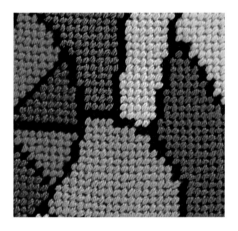

Tip When working with an even number of strands, six in this case, you can make a very neat beginning to a new thread. Cut a long length of stranded cotton (about 80cm/32in) and separate out three strands. Fold these in half and thread both ends into your needle, leaving the loop at the other end. Make the first tent stitch but leave the loop loose on the back. Pass the needle through the loop and pull so the stitch tightens – you will hardly see the join.

1 Prepare the canvas for work (see page 106) and follow the chart opposite.

2 Using six strands of stranded cotton (floss) work all the very dark brown outlines in tent stitch (see page 112). Fill in the shapes with diagonal tent stitch using the colours shown on the chart. Diagonal tent stitch distorts the canvas less and I think it is easier to work a more even tension and so your work will have a smoother finish.

Making up

1 Stretch the canvas to bring it back to square (see page 106). However carefully you have stitched, it will still have distorted a little and the stretching process will restore the shape and also even up your tension. Trim the bare canvas edge to 1.25cm (½in).

2 Make the bag by cutting the following pieces from the moiré satin:
two pieces 9 x 14cm (3½ x 5½in) for the side panels;
one piece 9 x 25cm (3½ x 10in) for the top front;
one piece 5 x 25cm (2 x 10in) for the bottom front;
one piece 23 x 25cm (9 x 10in) for the back;
one piece 13 x 25cm (5 x 10in) for the turn-over top;
two pieces 32 x 25cm (12½ x 10in) for the lining;
two pieces 7 x 100cm (2¾ x 39in) for handle straps, adjusting length to suit.

3 Sew the side panels to either side of the embroidery (see diagram below). Now sew the top front and the bottom front to the top and bottom of the embroidery and the side panels. This makes the bag front.

Bag front layout

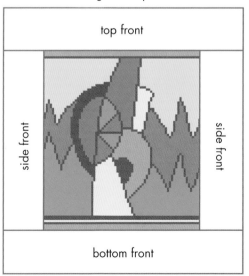

top front

side front

side front

bottom front

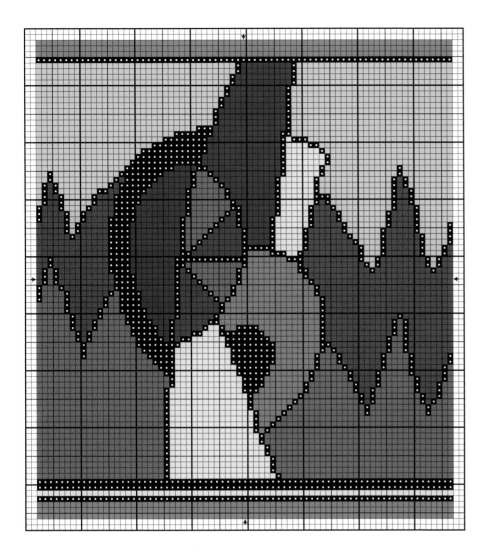

KEY Clarice Cliff Satchel

DMC stranded cotton

■	333	□	742	■	3721
□	676	■	900	■	3853
■	700	▣	3371		

4 Place the bag front and back right sides together and sew the sides and bottom. Trim this seam and turn right side out.

5 Make the handle straps by turning in the edges of the long pieces, folding in half and top stitching the edge. Top stitch the other edge to match. Sew the side seams of the turn-over top pieces.

6 Pin the straps in place at the top of the bag front, in line with the edges of the embroidered panel (see picture on page 21). Now put the turn-over top over the bag, right sides together, and sew around the top edge attaching the straps as you do this. Turn the turn-over top right side out and top stitch around the seam over the straps.

7 Sew the side seams of the lining, place the lining over the bag, right sides together, and sew around the top. Pull the lining right side out and above the bag. Turn the unfinished edges of the bottom of the lining in and top stitch along. Push the finished lining down inside the bag and top stitch the top of the bag to keep the lining in place. Turn the top over to be held in place by the straps. Finish by sewing on the brightly coloured buttons.

If you use brightly coloured buttons like these as a detail on your bag, sew them on with matching stranded cotton.

Lilac and Pearl Amulet

This amulet cube should hold something precious. I have a set of seed pearls with a pink hue to them and so the purse will hang on my dressing table with the pearls safe inside. It is said that pearls should be kept in silk so I have used a silk lining to keep them shiny. The threads are from a collection by Jean Oliver of Oliver Twists, and one skein has ten different thread types all space dyed in the same shades. They are available in a wonderful range of colours and I had great difficulty deciding which to use. I started another using shade, No.009, and the effect is very different (see overleaf). For the lilac and pearl bag there are three different squares and two of each make up the cube. The cords are from the same threads and one has a covered ring to close the top.

Finished bag size, excluding cord and tassel: 5.5cm (2¼in) cube

Tip You may find it helpful to draw six squares in pencil on the canvas to guide you as you place the squares next to each other. Use a fairly hard pencil that will not smudge and draw in between two threads of the canvas. Each square should enclose 26 canvas threads and the squares should have two canvas threads between them.

1 Begin by sorting the threads. When you undo the bundle you will find ten long lengths of different types of thread. The first four are braids that look as though they are knitted. Once you have identified the threads I suggest that you make ten thread winders out of card, wind the threads around them and label each with the numbers given below.

1	wide flat braid	6	matte twist
2	medium flat braid	7	very fine matte twist
3	fine flat braid	8	matte stranded cotton (use 6 strands)
4	round braid	9	cord with metallic
5	shiny twist	10	chenille (the fluffy one)

2 Prepare the canvas for work (see page 106) and follow the chart on page 29.

This embroidery is a work in progress using a different colourway from the Oliver Twists range (No.009). Before starting to stitch, I drew the six squares on my piece of canvas (see Tip above).

3 The cube is made up of three different squares each worked twice. The stitches used are tent stitch, backstitch, cross stitch, Rhodes stitch, rice stitch, satin stitch, long-legged cross stitch and French knots – see Stitches page 108.

SQUARE 1

- Work the four leaf shapes in straight stitches in the centre using thread 2.
- Work the row of tent stitch that joins these leaf tips in thread 5. Change the direction of the tent stitch at the tip of the leaves so all stitches in each quarter slant outwards.
- Work a second row of tent stitch outside the last, also in thread 5, leaving one canvas thread empty between the two rows.
- Fill the central area between the leaves and tent stitch line with tent stitch in thread 8, working the stitches in the same direction as the outer row.
- The row between the two rows of tent stitch is a strand of thread 10 couched down with straight stitches of thread 7. Bring the thick fluffy thread up through the canvas at the centre of one side, lay it in the line and couch it down all the way around the square. Pass the thick thread back down the same canvas hole that it came up – the join won't show.
- Work a row of cross stitch over two canvas threads in thread 9.
- Surround the square with a row of long-legged cross stitch in thread 3.

SQUARE 2

- Work a row of rice stitch around the outer edge of the square in thread 1 covered with thread 6. Note that in the middle of each side there are two cross stitches in thread 1 to make the pattern fit.
- Work the central area in zigzags of tent stitch in thread 9 and then satin stitch in thread 3.
- On the remaining canvas thread couch a row of thread 10 with thread 7 in the same way as you did in Square 1.

SQUARE 3

- Work the central Rhodes stitch in thread 9 and then the four that surround it in thread 3.
- Fill the small squares between the Rhodes stitch with tent stitch in thread 8. Direct the stitches towards the corner for each small square.
- Work the squares of satin stitch around the tent stitch and Rhodes stitch. The direction and threads alternate for each small square. Start in a corner with thread 3, with thread 8 for the others.
- Work a row of backstitch in thread 3 around the central area and then a French knot on each corner of the central Rhodes stitch.
- Work two rows of tent stitch one canvas thread apart to surround the square in thread 5.
- Couch a row of thread 10 with thread 7 between these two rows as before.

Now repeat all the squares, in the positions shown on the chart.

Square 1

Square 2

Square 3

Making up

1 Stretch the canvas piece to bring it back to square (see page 106). However carefully you have stitched it will still have distorted a little and the stretching process will restore the shape and even up your tension. Trim the bare canvas edges to 1.25cm (½in). Using the cross shape of the embroidered canvas as a pattern cut the same shape in lining fabric.

2 Work buttonhole stitch over the curtain ring to cover it (see picture below). Now cut a 182cm (72in) length of thread 4, twist it until it starts to double back on itself, thread it through the ring and allow the threads to twist to form a cord so you have a ring on the end of a cord. Knot the ends together. Make another cord twice as long by twisting 365cm (144in) of thread 4.

3 Make a tassel from 15 mixed threads cut to 15cm (6in) lengths – follow the general instructions in step 1 on page 67.

4 To make the cube shape, fold in all the canvas edges leaving one thread of canvas exposed as you fold up the squares. Work long-legged cross stitch in thread 8 on all the empty threads between the squares and on the joins of the box shape. Begin around the edge of the central square and on reaching the fourth corner, carry on up one side by taking one canvas thread from each folded-over edge for the long-legged cross stitch. As you work, tuck in the knotted end of the tassel at one corner, leaving the three seams opposite this corner open. Work a row of long-legged cross stitch around all the open edges.

5 Fold the long cord in half and, using matching thread, sew the ends to two of the corners at the top. Attach the end of the shorter cord with the loop on to the last corner.

6 Stitch the lining to fit inside the amulet and tuck inside. Turn the edges in and slipstitch down around the top edges of the cube.

7 To finish, tie the three cords together about halfway down and thread the loop over all three to slip down and hold the three top corners together.

The curtain ring, which closes the amulet, is covered with buttonhole stitch.

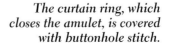

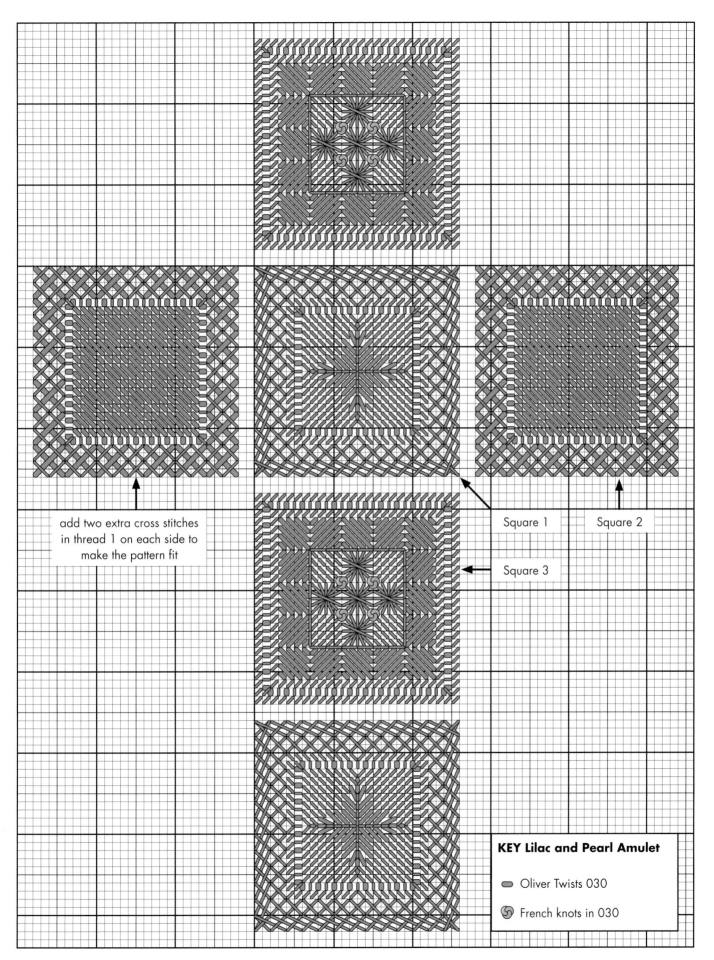

add two extra cross stitches
in thread 1 on each side to
make the pattern fit

Square 1

Square 2

Square 3

KEY Lilac and Pearl Amulet

Oliver Twists 030

French knots in 030

Peacock Beaded Purse

When my children were little we used to visit a bird park where there were lots of peacocks.
The girls would be amazed by the great shaking tails that went up as they approached. Then they
would be frightened by the birds' loud squawking cries. This tiny little peacock-inspired purse is
more a piece of jewellery than a useful bag but you could get a lipstick and credit card inside.
It's simply worked with iridescent seed beads and cross stitch on natural linen. I happened to
have a scrap of beautiful silk velvet in a deep peacock green colour which I used to back this purse.
Little treasured pieces of fabric like this are hard to come by but if you don't have one you
could always back your purse with the same silk that you use for the handle and the lining.

YOU WILL NEED

15 x 20cm (6 x 8in) 26-count natural linen

Size 24 tapestry needle and a beading needle

London Bead Company seed beads (see Suppliers) as listed in chart key

DMC stranded cotton (floss) 500 dark green

Strong beading thread in a neutral colour

25 x 25cm (10 x 10in) silk dupion for lining and handle

12 x 10cm (4¾ x 4in) silk velvet for backing

Gold-coloured metal purse top (see Suppliers)

Finished bag size, excluding fringe: 9 x 6cm (3½ x 2½in)

The beaded fringe completes this bag, giving it an opulent finish.

1 Prepare the linen for work (see page 106) and follow the chart opposite.

2 Begin at the top of the beaded area on the chart and work a row from left to right and then a second row from right to left and so on, attaching the beads with a beading needle, strong beading thread and half cross stitch (see page 113). Usually when working from a chart you work areas of colour but with beading you work in a single thread colour and build the design up one bead at a time in different colours. By working rows you will keep a more even tension on the beading thread and the beads will sit well (see Tip opposite).

3 Surround the beaded area with cross stitch in two strands of dark green stranded cotton (floss). This gives an edge that you can stitch right up to for the seam, as sewing close up to beads can be difficult.

Making up

1 Trim the excess fabric around the embroidery to 2cm (¾in). Using the embroidery as a pattern cut a piece for backing your purse and two pieces for the lining.

2 Place the front and back of the purse right sides together. Before sewing the seam, offer the pieces up to the metal purse top and mark where the seam should end.

3 Sew the two lining pieces together to match. Trim the purse seam and the lining and turn the purse right sides out. Tuck the lining into the purse. Turn in the top edges of the purse and lining and tack (baste) together to hold in place. Using two strands of stranded cotton and backstitch, attach the purse

top over the top of the embroidery and the backing. There is no clever way to do this because you cannot pin metal so just do it carefully.

4 To make and attach the beaded fringe begin in the middle of the bottom edge. Thread a long length of beading thread in the beading needle and bring it out at the centre bottom. Thread on 6 dark green beads then 16 golden brown ones and finally 4 bronze. Now, missing out the last bronze bead on the thread, take the needle back through all the other beads thus ending up back at the edge of the purse. Repeat this sequence of beads all the way up one edge until the strings of beads stop hanging next to each other smoothly, then make the last few strings progressively shorter towards the end. Repeat the fringe up the other side to match.

5 To finish, make a handle out of a fine tube of lining fabric (see step 3 on page 36) or use a fine chain or a string of mixed beads.

Tip I find beading easier with the fabric stretched on a frame because it is then possible to keep the beading thread tight between the beads so they sit more neatly on the fabric.

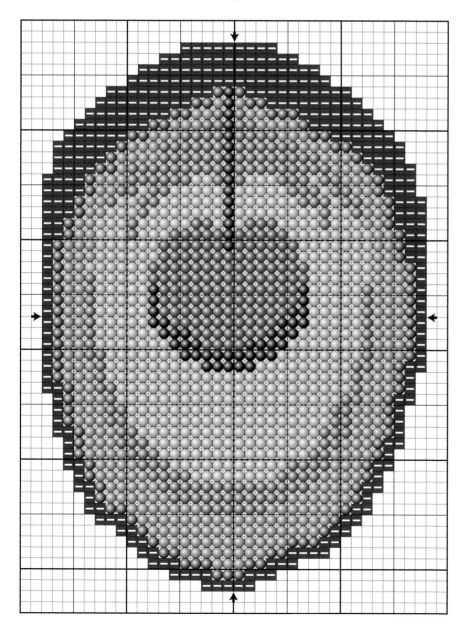

KEY Peacock Beaded Purse

London Bead Company seed beads
(1 packet of each colour)

● 054 dark green
● 552 dark purple
● 546 bright blue
○ 567 bright peacock
● 601 bronze
● 4341 light green
○ 4344 golden brown

DMC stranded cotton
▬ 500 (cross stitch)

Flying Carpet Bag

This simple little bag can take you all over the world. It is just the right size to hold your passport and tickets as you pass through an airport and is slim enough to wear under your jacket to keep all your important travel documents safe and out of sight. No more desperate rummaging through hand luggage stuffed with stitching and paperback books at the check-in desk. I have used really bright colours but you could tone them down a little by choosing softer, more muted, shades. The pattern is worked in tent stitch with an edging of long-legged cross stitch and is based on an antique rug so it will look just as good stitched in more subtle colours. Refer to Stitches pages 108–113 for how to work the stitches used.

Finished bag size, excluding handles: 16 x 12.5cm (6¼ x 5in)

1 Prepare the canvas for work (see page 106) and follow the chart opposite.

2 Working from the centre of the chart in tent stitch and with two strands of 934 deep mauve crewel wool, outline the central medallion shapes.

3 Fill the shapes with diagonal tent stitch. The blue, gold and red are all mixed colours for a muted antique look, so use one strand of each colour in the needle. Stitch the perlé thread with one strand last, so you don't take the sheen off the thread as you handle it.

4 Work the red outlines in the outer corners and then fill in the gold background and perlé shapes. Work the triple-row striped border and then a row of deep mauve long-legged cross stitch around the whole edge.

Making up

1 Stretch the canvas to bring it back to square (see page 106). Trim the bare canvas edge to 1.25cm (½in).

2 Using the finished embroidery as a pattern, cut out three pieces of silk – one for backing and two for lining.

3 To make a handle, cut enough 3cm (1¼in) wide bias strips for a handle as long as you require plus an extra 9cm (3½in) to make a button loop, and join the strips together. To cut on the true bias, fold the selvedge of the fabric to the straight grain widthwise and then cut along the fold. Fold the bias strip in half lengthwise and sew a seam to create a tube 1cm (⅜in) wide. Trim the seam and turn the tube inside out so the seam is now on the inside (see the Tip opposite). Alternatively, thread a thick needle with a short thread and catch it into the end of the tubing. Pass the needle down through the tube and out the other end. Start the end of the tube turning and then pull the first end right through the whole tube. Cut off a 9cm (3½in) length to make the button loop and set aside for the moment.

4 Place the embroidery right sides together with the piece of backing fabric and stitch around both sides and the bottom. Stitch right against the embroidery using the same set of canvas holes as the last row of embroidery so that no canvas shows.

The button loop and handle, made in the same fabric as the backing, give this bag a professional-looking finish.

5 Take the two pieces of silk for the lining and stitch them together down the sides only.

6 Check the length of the handle and pin it to either side of the bag at the top edge. Pin the button loop to the centre top of the embroidered front. Place the lining over the bag on the outside with the right sides together and sew around the top edge. Pull the lining up, sew across the bottom and push the lining down inside the bag.

7 Sew the button on the back of the bag, at the top. Put your passport and tickets inside and off you go on a wonderful holiday!

Tip Most good haberdashers or craft stores sell a tool designed for making tubing: it is a long metal wire with a loop to hold at one end and a clever little latch hook at the other for seizing the end of the tube.

KEY Flying Carpet Bag

Appletons crewel wool (Mute the colours by using a mixture of two shades)

Golds 694 + 695

Blues 749 + 926

Reds 866 + 725

Deep mauve 934

DMC perlé cotton No.5

976

Bags with Attitude

These two bags, pink sparkles and black zips as I call them, are the same size and shape but very different in feel. The most difficult thing about them is assembling a goodly collection of haberdashery and trimmings. If you do a lot of stitching you probably have some bits already but if you don't, then start collecting now – don't forget junk shops and jumble sales where you can find interesting old items that are no longer made. The sparkly beaded trim on the pink bag is a remnant of beaded lampshade trimming and the little chain lengths on the black bag are for stitching into a coat collar (to hang the coat on). Look at all the bits and pieces in those little packets in the haberdashery section and give them new functions.

Finished bag size (each):
19 x 25cm (7½ x 10in)

Tip If you have a digital camera, take a picture of the bag front once you have laid out all the bits and pieces and are happy with your composition. Then you can take it all apart to sew on the different layers but will still have a picture to refer to as you go. If you don't have a camera, make a sketch.

1 Make a paper pattern of all the pieces using the templates on pages 114–115 and then cut out all the pieces. Note: the top facing and front and back templates are too large too produce in full, so place the marked fold line on a fold in your fabric to cut out a complete piece.

2 Take the bag front and lay it right side up on your table, assemble all your trimmings and fabric scraps and make a collage to decorate your bag. I've used a piece of contrasting fabric on both bags stitched on diagonally, tucking in one side of the zip on the black bag and the tape of the lampshade trim on the pink bag. A diagonal line like this seems to break up the shape and makes it easier to assemble a good arrangement of bits. Cover the colour with lace if you have some and add the trimmings in layers and overlap them. On the black bag I used beads to attach the hooks and chains and added a hammer-on metal stud button near the bottom. An old diamante brooch pinned on also adds more sparkle.

Making up

1 Find the centre of one of the long sides of the gusset and the centre of the bottom of the bag front. Match these two points together and, with the bag front and gusset right sides together, pin the gusset to the bag front – the pointed ends of the gusset will finish before the top of the sides. Sew this seam. Attach the back of the bag in the same way. Sew the back to the front above the gusset on each side. Make the lining in exactly the same way as the bag. Now sew the short sides of the bag, facing right sides together.

2 Take two of the bag handle pieces, place them right sides together and sew the long side seams. Turn right sides out and top stitch the seams to keep them in place. Repeat for the other pieces to make four handle holders. Fold these in half and pin to the top outside edges of the bag.

3 Place the top facing over the bag and handle holders right sides together and sew the top seam. Turn the top facing into the top of the bag, making the handle holders all stand up. Catch the top facing down to the inside of the bag to hold it in place. Tuck the lining inside the bag, turn over the top edge and slipstitch in place.

4 Spray paint the dowelling (see Tip, right). Once the dowelling is dry, measure the length you need to fill the handle holders right to the sides and cut two lengths. Sew channels in the top of the handle holders and slip the dowel into these. To finish, hand stitch the ends of the channels on the outer edges to hold the dowelling in place.

Tip Paint more dowelling than you need and cut it afterwards so that you have a bit to hold on to as you spray. Spray outside on a still, dry day and make sure the wood is completely dry before you cut it to size or get it anywhere near your lovely bag. I stuck the end that I had been holding into the earth while the painted end dried.

Tooth Fairy and Elf

These two tiny bags are great fun. I made the fairy first and then thought that there should be something for boys and so her rather lumpy little boyfriend came into being. My daughters are both grown up now but I still remember the excitement of the first teeth to come out and the notes written to the tooth fairy. She used the teeth to build fairy castles in our house. These funny characters hang on the bedstead and carry a linen bag for the tooth – you could backstitch their names on the bags. All you have to do then is remember to remove the tooth and replace it with a coin – it used to be a silver sixpence but I imagine inflation has hit tooth fairies as well as the rest of us. The fairy and elf are 12cm (4¾in) from head to toe and are shown here larger than actual size.

Shoe template
Cut 4 from white felt (actual size)

Stitching the fairy

1 Prepare the canvas for work (see page 106) and follow the fairy chart on the lower part of page 47 to work the little rectangle of canvas using six strands of stranded cotton and four strands of the gold lamé for the satin stitch, rice stitch and long-legged cross stitch (see Stitches page 108).

2 Stretch this tiny piece of work by pressing it carefully on the wrong side with a steam iron and pulling it gently back to shape.

3 Stitch the bag design on the linen, over two threads, following the top left chart on page 47. Work the cross stitch with one strand. You could add the words 'Tooth Fairy' in backstitch in two strands (see caption opposite). Work the hem-stitched edge.

4 To make the little bag trim the linen to the edge of the hem stitching, fold in half and stitch the sides together. Make tiny handles from twisted cords (see step 1 below) made with three strands of stranded cotton 7cm (2¾in) long. Tie knots in each end of the handles and stitch these knots to the outside of the linen bag.

Making up the fairy

1 Make the legs and arms by first cutting twelve 30cm (12in) lengths of pink stranded cotton (Anchor 1021). Twist three of these together tightly, fold in half so a cord is formed and knot the two ends to prevent unravelling. Repeat three more times. Separate out the twist at the end of all these cords to make hands and feet. Tie knots to make knobbly knees in two and shorten the other two to make arms. Cut four tiny shoes from a scrap of white felt (see below left for template) and glue to either side of the feet. Trim with seed beads.

2 Trim the empty canvas around the embroidery to 1cm (⅜in) and turn all edges in. Join the two short edges of the oblong together using long-legged cross stitch. Work from the right side taking one canvas thread from each side of the join to work the stitches over. This is the back seam of the dress. Work a join across the bottom of the dress, tucking in the legs as you go.

3 Fill the dress with polyester filling and gather up the top as best you can, tucking an arm into each shoulder and oversewing the seam.

4 Draw a simple face on the bead with a black pen and add rosy cheeks with spots of nail varnish.

5 Make a twisted cord using the six strands of stranded cotton. Take about twelve 15cm (6in) lengths of the white perlé cotton (the number varies depending on the size of the bead hole) and lay the twisted cord with them. Fold all this in half and make a loop of stranded cotton around the centre of the bundle. Now thread both ends of the stranded cotton through the bead and pull a loop of the cord and perlé cotton through the bead – tight enough so her head stands up. The loop you've pulled through should just show at the bottom of the bead and becomes her neck. Sew the head on to the body and separate out all the threads of the perlé cotton for hair.

6 Cut rounded ends on the piece of net. Gather up the centre and stitch the wings to her back. Hang the tooth bag over her shoulder and secure with a stitch. Make a wand from the two stars and the pin and trim with bits of feather and a bead. Poke the pin through her hands into the dress to finish.

While the tooth fairy will always be a favourite with little girls, the tooth elf provides a more masculine alternative for the boys. There is a space in the centre of each linen bag to add their names, 'Tooth Fairy' or 'Tooth Elf' (or other names of your choice). Use two strands of thread and backstitch and the alphabet charted on page 47.

Finished elf size, body only:
12cm (4¾in)

Stitching the elf

The stitching and making up for the elf is very similar to the fairy so refer to steps 1–4 on page 44 but use the elf charts opposite. Change the stitching colours at the central line on the chart – green multicolour one side, red on the other.

Making up the elf

1 The colours of the elf's legs and arms are different to the fairy but follow the instructions for the fairy and use the picture to help you. Add gold bead buttons to his front. Work a backstitch edge to his belt and a buckle with one strand of lamé thread. Make up the bag as for the fairy.

2 Make the hat and hair by gluing a few strands of brown stranded cotton to the top of his head before you glue the hat on. For the hat, cut two triangles in red felt (see below for templates). Stitch them together around the two top edges leaving a gap for the cord to pass through. Make the hat around the cord and glue it to the bead head over the hair. Cut a green zigzag-topped piece and glue this to the bottom edge of the hat. Sew a gold bead to the hat tip. Place the ruff around his neck and catch it in place with a few stitches.

3 To finish, cut out his boots from felt, glue them either side of his feet and sew gold beads to the points.

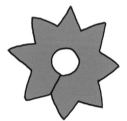

Neck ruff template
Cut 1 from red felt (actual size)

Hat template
Cut 2 from red felt (actual size)

Hat trim template
Cut 1 from green felt (actual size)

Boots template
Cut 2 from red felt and 2 from green (actual siz

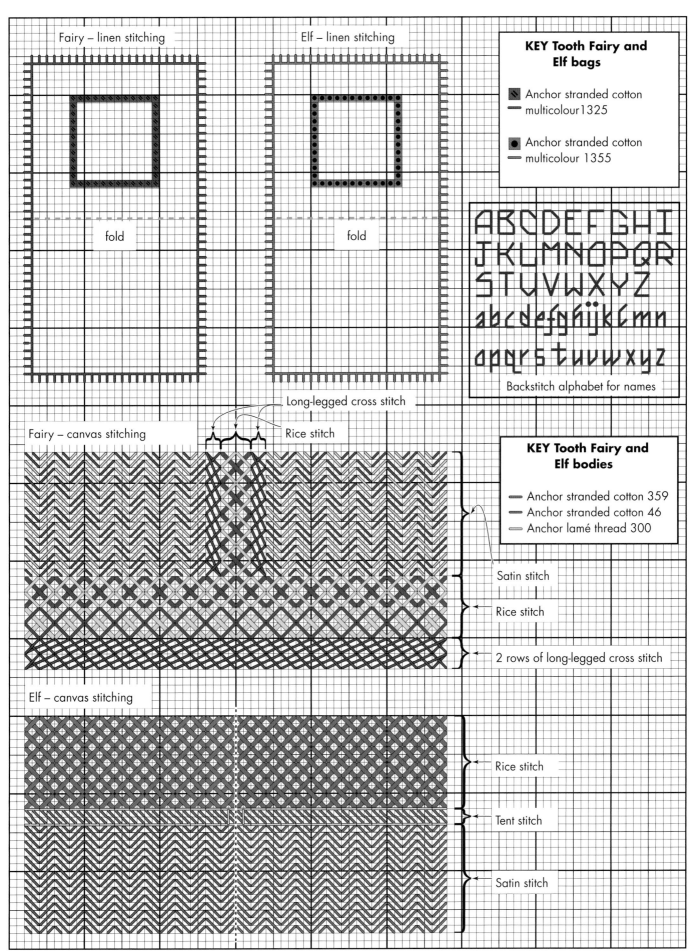

Fairy – linen stitching

Elf – linen stitching

fold

fold

KEY Tooth Fairy and Elf bags

▨ Anchor stranded cotton
— multicolour 1325

● Anchor stranded cotton
— multicolour 1355

A B C D E F G H I
J K L M N O P Q R
S T U V W X Y Z
a b c d e f g h i j k l m n
o p q r s t u v w x y z

Backstitch alphabet for names

Long-legged cross stitch

Rice stitch

Fairy – canvas stitching

KEY Tooth Fairy and Elf bodies

━ Anchor stranded cotton 359
━ Anchor stranded cotton 46
━ Anchor lamé thread 300

Satin stitch

Rice stitch

2 rows of long-legged cross stitch

Elf – canvas stitching

Rice stitch

Tent stitch

Satin stitch

African Animal Bag

I had a very special trip to Kenya with my family and this animal-inspired bag is the result of that memorable trip to Africa. All the patterns are traced from some of my many photographs taken in the amazing Masai Mara game reserve. We had a long, hot day there in a big open-topped jeep and I ended up with a very sunburned face but with a wonderful set of pictures. We were very lucky to see a cheetah and a leopard; giraffe and zebra, of course, were there in their hundreds. The snake pattern I've used on the bag was actually from a huge python we saw in a snake farm nearby and the little gecko crawled across the roof of our tent one night. The deep red edging I've used on the bag was inspired by the red soil of the region.

Finished bag size, excluding strap and tassel: 20 x 19.5cm (8 x 7¾in)

Tip Tweeding threads, that is working two or more colours together in the needle, not only gives you a wider colour palette but, in the case of the animal designs on this bag, breaks up solid areas of colour in a more natural way, making the patterns appear far more subtle and convincing.

1 Prepare the canvas for work (see page 106) and follow the chart opposite. Begin with the beaded gecko. Work in horizontal rows attaching each bead with a half cross stitch (see page 113) and beading thread, with three dark metallic blue beads for each eye.

2 Work the deep red dividing lines in tent stitch using six strands of stranded cotton. Fill in the patterns in each section in tent stitch. Some of the colours use three strands of two colours to soften the shades (see chart key). Finally, work a row of long-legged cross stitch in deep red along the straight top edge.

Making up

1 Stretch the canvas to bring it back to square (see page 106). Trim bare canvas edges to 1.25cm (½in).

2 Using the embroidery as a pattern, cut one piece of leather or backing fabric and two in lining. Place the embroidery and backing right sides together and stitch around the curved edges close to the edge. Trim and clip the seam and turn right sides out. Turn over the top edges and turn over the backing to match. Catch these edges down loosely to the wrong side.

3 Stitch the lining pieces together right sides together. Push the lining into the bag, fold over the top edges and slipstitch in place.

4 To make the twisted cord for an edging and handle, take eight 4m (4⅓yd) lengths of stranded cotton. (Each skein of thread is 8m long so you need four skeins undone and cut in half.) Take four of these lengths and twist until the thread begins to double back on itself when you release the tension slightly. Fold in half and let go of the centre point gradually, holding the two ends together. Knot the ends together. Take the other four lengths to make a second cord but thread the second through the loop of the first to make a long cord. Twist and fold one final time to make a double-twisted cord. Make the cord into a loop by knotting the ends, leaving a 5cm (2in) tail.

6 Place the knot of the looped cord against the pointed bottom of the bag and slipstitch in place, up the edge and finishing off well at the top. Repeat for the second side. To finish, trim the tassel ends and separate out the threads.

Tip I backed my bag with a lovely piece of glove leather I'd been treasuring. Unfortunately it wasn't quite wide enough so I had to seam it. When I finished I actually liked the seam so if you have a problem sometimes it can be made into a feature that adds to the piece.

KEY African Animal Bag

DMC stranded cotton
(Some colours are created by
mixing three strands each of
two colours in the needle)

Mill Hill Petite Glass beads

	DMC		
▨	301 + 435	⊙	3031
▨	435 + 729	▨	3032
▨	632 + 839	·	3033
▢	677 + 729	▨	3771
▨	841	▨	3777 (6 skeins)
▨	3021	▢	ecru

🔘 40556 brass
🔘 40374 metallic blue

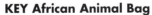

Floral Wedding

Family and friends are all there, it's a beautiful summer day in the countryside, a marquee is set on the sweeping lawns of an old country house, posies of wild flowers are on the tables with simple fare and plenty of sparkling champagne! Here are bags for the bride to fill with 'something old, something new, something borrowed and something blue' and two bridesmaids' bags to match. The bride has a pretty drawstring dolly bag, while the older bridesmaid's bag is a simple fold-over purse attached to a ruched, silk-covered bangle so that she has her hands free to catch the bouquet. The youngest bridesmaid follows with a little purse on a string. You could also embroider some of the little sprigs of flowers on to the name cards at the tables or use them on the invitations.

Bride's Dolly Bag

1 Prepare the linen for work and stitch the motif from the chart on page 56, repeating it three times – the dashed blue lines show the repeat. Cross stitch over two fabric threads using two strands of stranded cotton.

2 Press the finished embroidery with plenty of steam right side down on two layers of towel, to avoid flattening the stitches.

Making up

1 Trim the linen strip to 7cm (2⅜in) wide, centring the embroidery. Cut silk the same size for a lining. Stitch the short edges of the embroidery together into a tube. Seam the lining in the same way and slip inside the embroidery. Tack (baste) the lining to the embroidery to hold the two together.

2 Cut a circle of stiffening 12cm (4¾in) in diameter and two in silk for the base. Tack the stiffening between the silk layers. Pin the base to the bottom edge of the lined embroidery tube leaving the seam on the outside – clip the edge carefully to do this. Sew this seam and trim to about 7mm (¼in).

3 Bind the edges with bias binding (see page 107) or use purchased binding. Machine stitch on the right side, turn over the edge and slipstitch down.

4 To make the bag top cut two silk pieces 18 x 28cm (7 x 11in) and seam together along the short sides. Gather the bottom to fit the top edge of the embroidery and pin wrong sides together, seam outside. Stitch and bind this seam as for the bottom edge. Turn the top edge by 3.5cm (1⅜in) and machine down on the edge. Stitch a second row 1cm (⅜in) away from the first row to make a casing and create a frill. Cut the side seam between the two rows of stitching to make an opening on each side.

5 To make the drawstring ties, cut enough 4cm (1½in) wide bias strips to make two 70cm (27½in) ties and join them together. Fold the bias strip in half lengthwise and sew a seam to make a 1cm (⅜in) wide tube (or use purchased satin binding). Trim the seam and turn the tube inside out so the seam is on the inside (see Tip on page 37). Turn in the unfinished ends and hand sew.

6 Thread one tie through the casing and knot the ends together. Thread the other tie from the opposite side and knot it. To finish, tie bows on top of the knots to make a pretty detail.

Bride's Dolly Bag
YOU WILL NEED

12 x 46cm (4¾ x 18in)
28-count ivory linen

Size 26 tapestry needle

DMC stranded cotton (floss)
as listed in chart key

40cm (16in) ivory silk dupion
for making up

Scrap of pelmet stiffening or
heavy Vilene for the base
(or soft card)

Ivory satin binding (optional) or
silk dupion for bias strips

Finished bag size, excluding handle: 17 x 12cm (6¾ x 4¾in)

Bridesmaid's Bangle Bag

1 The two bridesmaids' bags are made in the same way, only the handles and sizes differ. Prepare the linen for work and start from the centre of the designs charted on page 57. Cross stitch over two fabric threads using two strands of stranded cotton.

2 Press the embroidery as you did for step 2 of the dolly bag opposite.

Making up

1 Trim the embroidery and sew it to the shorter piece of silk. Make a sandwich of the lining, wadding and embroidery. Pin the layers together and cut a rounded end to the embroidery. Stitch the layers together around the edges.

2 Bind the straight edge, as in step 3 of the dolly bag, and then fold the bag so the pocket is a little longer than the flap. Pin the edges together.

3 Take the strips of silk for the handle and the bangle. Fold in half lengthwise and make a seam. Trim the seam and turn right sides out. Take the shorter one, thread the piping cord through it, gather the silk to fit the cord and stitch the ends. Thread the other on to the bangle, gathering it to fit. Tape the ends of the break in the bangle together with adhesive tape and slipstitch the ends of the silk tube together. Thread the corded length through the bangle and pin the ends to the back of the bag at the top.

4 Sew the binding on the bag from one corner, around the flap to the other corner, attaching the bangle as you go.

5 Make a buttonhole loop (see page 108) to fit your button in the middle of the flap and sew the button in place to finish.

Bridesmaid's Bangle Bag

YOU WILL NEED

20 x 25cm (8 x 10in) 28-count ivory linen

Size 26 tapestry needle

DMC stranded cotton (floss) as listed in chart key

16 x 40cm (6¼ x 16in) polyester wadding (batting)

Mother-of-pearl button, with shank rather than holes

A bangle (with a break in it to cover it neatly – cut through a cheap plastic one)

Silk pieces as follows:
one 17 x 40cm (6¾ x 15¾in);
one 17 x 30cm (6¾ x 12in);
one 4 x 30cm (1½ x 12in);
one 4 x 38cm (1½ x 15in)
to cover bangle

Polyester wadding (batting) 17 x 40cm (6¾ x 15¾in)

Enough 3cm (1¼in) wide bias strips to make 1m (39in) of binding or 1m (39in) of purchased satin bias binding

15cm (6in) of piping cord

Finished bag size, excluding handle: 13.5 x 17cm (5½ x 6¾in)

Bridesmaid's Purse

YOU WILL NEED

15 x 15cm (6 x 6in) 28-count ivory linen

Size 26 tapestry needle

DMC stranded cotton (floss) as listed in chart key

10 x 30cm (4 x 12in) polyester wadding (batting)

Mother-of-pearl button, with shank not holes

Silk pieces as follows:
one 10 x 25cm (4 x 10in);
one 10 x 18cm (4 x 7in)

Polyester wadding (batting)
10 x 25cm (4 x 10in)

Enough 3cm (1¼in) wide bias strips to make 130cm (51in) of binding or 130cm (51in) of purchased satin bias binding

Finished bag size, excluding handle: 8.5 x 9cm (3½ x 3½in)

Bridesmaid's Purse

1 Follow steps 1 and 2 of the bangle bag on page 55 to work the embroidery, Trim the embroidery and sew it to the shorter piece of silk. Make a sandwich of the lining, wadding (batting) and embroidery. Pin the layers together and cut a rounded end to the embroidery. Stitch the layers together around the edge.

2 Bind the straight edge, as in step 3 of the dolly bag, and fold the purse so the pocket is a little longer than the flap. Pin the edges together. Cut a 70cm (27½in) length of bias strip or purchased satin binding, Fold it lengthwise right sides together and sew the seam. Turn right side out. Adjust the length of this strap depending on the size of the bridesmaid. Pin one end to each side of the back of the purse. Now bind from one corner all around the flap and finish at the other corner attaching the strap as you go.

3 Finally, make a buttonhole loop (see page 108) to fit your button and sew the button on under the flap, in the middle.

Dolly Bag

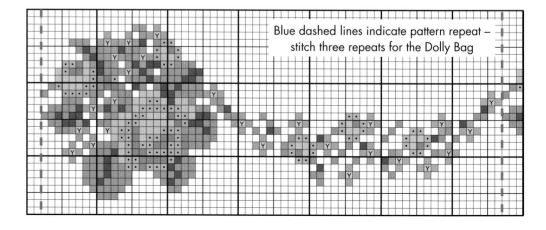

Blue dashed lines indicate pattern repeat – stitch three repeats for the Dolly Bag

Bangle Bag

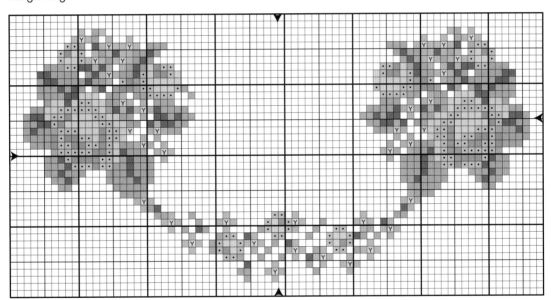

KEY Floral Wedding

DMC stranded cotton

Y 676

• 758

948

3012

3013

3042

3778

Purse

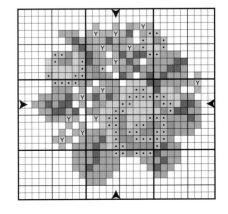

Harlequin Lily

This glamorous bag looks complicated but, taken step by step, it is not as difficult as you might think – and it is made from easily obtainable bits and pieces. The petals of the impressive three-dimensional lily are stiffened with wire so they can be bent into soft shapes, and the lily's flowing lines contrast well with the regular squares of the canvaswork embroidery on the bag. The bag is worked in lustrous space-dyed threads, so it looks sophisticated even though I have only used two colours. You could easily change the colours of the bag or the lily (or both) to suit your evening dress. Try out a colour change on some spare canvas before you start. You could also make just the lily for a pretty corsage. Refer to Stitches (pages 108–113) for the stitches used.

Finished bag size, excluding handle: 14 x 15.5cm (5½ x 6in)

Stitching the lily

1 Iron the Vilene on to the back of your fabric. This will stiffen your petals a little and also help to prevent fraying when they are cut out.

2 Trace the petal and leaf outlines given opposite on to tracing paper using a black felt-tip pen. Lay the stiffened fabric over the tracing. The outline should show through the fabric enough for you to be able to trace it. (A sheet of white paper under the tracing will show up the lines more clearly.)

3 Petals 1, 3 and 5 are worked in ecru and light gold. Petals 2, 4 and 6 are worked in light gold and dark gold. Outline each petal in split backstitch first, using three strands of either ecru or light gold. This split backstitch won't show once the stitching is finished but provides a slightly raised edge to the petals which makes it much easier to line up the ends of the all your long and short stitches.

Tip When working with stranded cotton (floss) always separate out the strands one by one and then recombine them to stitch. This removes the twist and gives a really smooth finish.

4 Using three strands of stranded cotton (floss) fill the petals with long and short stitch using the lighter colour on the outer edge. It is easier to come up through the fabric on the outside of the split backstitch and down towards the centre of the petal. Work the second row from the centre vein outwards. A long stitch should alternate with a short one but don't be too rigid about this. Imagine that you are painting and that the stitches are random brush strokes on the canvas. When working long and short stitch always split the threads of each successive layer of stitching, to ensure a good blending of colour and smooth stitches. Your stitches should be longer than feels necessary because they will be shortened by the following layer of stitches. As you work, be aware of the direction of each thread that you lay on the fabric, making sure the stitches of the next layer lie in the same direction as the first.

5 Work the veins on the petals in stem stitch using three strands of mauve. To finish the petal, use two strands of mauve to scatter French knots over each petal (see picture, right).

Tip For your lily petals, choose a cotton fabric that is closely woven enough to support the weight of the embroidery but fine enough not to add excessive thickness.

6 Work the leaf in long and short stitch in the same way as the petals but in light green. Add a dark green stem-stitched vein down the centre.

7 Edge all the petals with fuse wire by cutting a length of wire at least 5cm (2in) longer than the perimeter of each petal and attaching it with buttonhole stitch using two strands of either ecru or light gold stranded cotton (floss). Bend up 2.5cm (1in), leave this at the beginning, work all round the petal and then leave another 2.5cm (1in) length at the finish, next to where you started. Edge the leaf in the same way. You will use these loose bits of wire to push through the canvas and attach the petals to the bag front.

8 Very carefully cut out the six petals and the leaf, cutting first to within about 7mm (¼in) then trimming right down. Use really sharp little scissors and cut closely under the coil of the buttonhole stitch. Twist the wires of each petal to make a stem and trim to about 2cm (¾in).

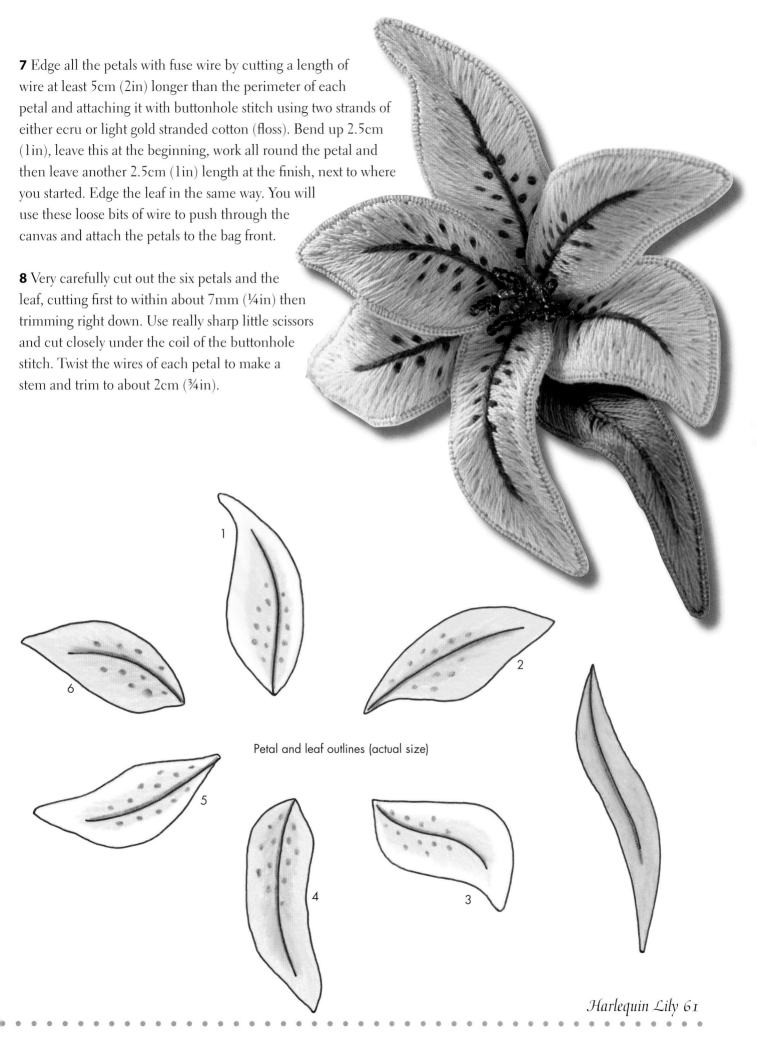

1

6

2

Petal and leaf outlines (actual size)

5

4

3

Harlequin Lily 61

Stitching the bag

1 Lay the canvas over the bag front and back template on page 117. Draw the shape of the bag twice on the canvas with black felt-tip, omitting the leaves on the back piece.

2 Work the leaves in long and short stitch in light green, filling to the mid line, and finish with a stem stitch vein in dark green. Leave an empty space in the centre of the leaves to poke wires through from the petals.

3 Work the cushion stitch squares (satin stitch) on the rest of the bag front, fitting the squares around the leaves. Use two strands of the Tudor Twist thread. Make sure the colour changes match on both strands or you will mix up the colours and produce a tweeded effect rather than a progression of colour. Work each full cushion stitch square over four canvas threads in each direction, as shown in the chart opposite, in alternate colours with the diagonal stitches in alternate directions. Begin with one full square in rainbow at the centre of the top curve of the shape and the rest will fall into place as you work.

4 Work cushion stitch to fill the shape for the bag back.

Making up

1 Poke the twisted wires of the leaf through the canvas in the centre of the leaves and then bend the twist so that it lies flat to the back of the canvas. Add all the petals in the same way. This is a bit fiddly because you have quite a lot of wires going through very close to each other. Do them one at a time and bend each out of the way. Catch the twists with small stitches to the back of the embroidery to hold the petals in place. Arrange the flower so that the three darker petals sit in the front of the lighter ones.

2 Add a cluster of beaded stamens to the centre of the flower. Thread one strand of stranded cotton (floss) in the beading needle and push it up through the canvas in the centre of the flower, thread on six gold seed beads and three mauve beads. Now thread back through the second seed bead and all the rest and down though the canvas again, pulling tightly. The stamen will stand up. Make four more in the same way.

3 To prevent the wires on the back of the flower piercing through the silk lining of your bag, cut a small square of felt to cover these wires and sew it carefully to the back of the embroidery. Any felt colour will do as it will not show once the lining is stitched into place.

4 Cut out the embroidered shapes leaving a 7mm (¼in) margin of bare canvas. Lay both on the silk dupion and cut out exactly the same shapes for the lining.

5 Cut out the gusset shape (on page 117) in canvas, and cut the same shape twice in silk dupion. Note: half the pattern is given.

6 Pin the linings to the front and back of the bag and then to either side of the gusset. Stitch close to the edge around all these pieces to keep the linings in place. Bend the wired petals carefully out of the way as you do this.

7 Cut 4cm (1½in) wide bias-cut strips from the remaining silk dupion. To cut on the true bias so the binding will be stretchy and curve easily, fold the selvedge of the fabric to the straight grain widthways and cut along the fold. You will need two 80cm (32in) lengths and two 5cm (2in) lengths.

8 Use the two short pieces to bind the short ends of the gusset. Sew the right sides together on one side and trim the seam to 7mm (¼in). Turn the binding to the wrong side, turn it under and slipstitch it down (see Tip, right). Trim the excess at each end.

9 Pin the gusset to one side of the bag, wrong sides together, and sew with the seam on the outside of the bag. You will need to ease the curves of the side on to the straighter side of the gusset and match the points to the bound short edges of the gusset. Repeat for the other side.

10 Find the mid point of one 80cm (32in) length of bias-cut strip and pin it to the mid point of the bottom of the outside of one side of the bag. Now pin the binding over the seam that is sticking out, leaving trailing ends at each end to make the handles. Sew the strip on and then turn the binding to the gusset side. Turn it under and pin in place.

11 You now have four ends of bias strips trailing off the top of the bag. These need seaming together to make the handles. Adjust the lengths to match each other exactly, to the length you prefer. Turn in both edges of the handles to match the width of the binding around the bag and pin. To finish your bag, hand stitch the handles and binding all the way around and remove the pins.

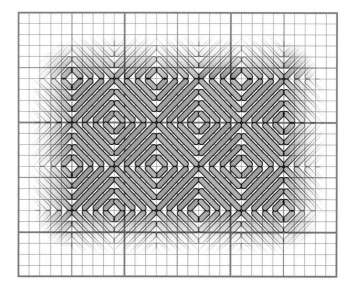

KEY Harlequin Lily

De Havilland Tudor Twist

 mauve/pink

 rainbow

Note: the chart shows a small section of the repeating design. Space-dyed threads are shown as a single colour for clarity.

Tip To attach bias binding you can either machine first on the wrong side and then top stitch down on the right side as I did, or if you are nervous about machining a perfectly straight line, machine on the right side and then slipstitch on the wrong side. See page 107.

Miser's Purse

The opening in this funny little purse is in the middle between the two beaded rings. It's only by sliding the rings to each side that you can get into the purse. It is called a miser's purse because it is difficult to get into. You will often find old examples of this type of purse in museum collections and I thought I'd like to make a modern version. I chose pure silk thread to knit with – a lovely space-dyed thread really intended for embroidery but by knitting it you can really see the beautiful colour changes. The addition of beads in the knitting and encrusted on the rings, plus a tassel on each end made it much more glamorous and I shall use it for precious jewellery. I found a scrap of pale gold Habotai silk to line the purse but you could leave it unlined.

The Thread Gatherer Silken
Pearl (see Suppliers), three
skeins 15/3 morning glory and
one skein 30/3 morning glory

Pair 3mm knitting needles
(US size 2–3)

One packet Mill Hill size 6
glass beads 16609

One packet Mill Hill
seed beads 02045

Two 2.5cm (1in) diameter
plastic curtain rings

Fine strong thread for beading

Beading needle and
a tapestry needle

24 x 16cm (9½ x 6¼in) silk
for lining (optional)

*Finished bag size, excluding
tassels: 4 x 21cm (1½ x 8¼in)*

Tip To achieve a firm edge to
your knitting, which you want for
the opening of the purse, slip the
first stitch of every row instead
of knitting or purling it.

Open a skein of the thicker thread (15/3) and wind it into a ball or around a piece of card. Thread about half of the size 6 beads on to it so you can knit them in when you come to that bit – for now just leave them on the thread and push them along as you come to them.

1 Cast on 6 stitches.
2 Increase into each of these stitches by knitting into the front and then the back of each of them. (12 stitches)
3 Slip 1 stitch and purl to the end.
4 Slip 1 stitch, increase into the next stitch, (knit 1, increase into the next stitch). Repeat sequence in brackets to end of row. (18 stitches)
5 Slip 1 stitch and purl to the end.
6 Slip 1 stitch, knit 1, increase into the next stitch, (knit 2, increase into the next stitch). Repeat sequence in brackets to end of row. (24 stitches)
7 Slip 1 stitch and purl to the end.
8 Slip 1 stitch, knit 2, increase into the next stitch, (knit 3, increase into the next stitch). Repeat sequence in brackets to end of row. (30 stitches)
9 Slip 1 stitch and purl to the end.
10 Slip 1 stitch, knit 3, increase into the next stitch, (knit 4, increase into the next stitch). Repeat sequence in brackets to end of row. (36 stitches)
11 Slip 1 stitch and purl to the end.
12 Slip 1 stitch, knit 4, increase into the next stitch, (knit 5, increase into the next stitch). Repeat sequence in brackets to end of row. (42 stitches)

13 Slip 1 stitch and purl to the end.
14 Slip 1 stitch, knit 5, increase into the next stitch, (knit 6, increase into the next stitch). Repeat sequence in brackets to end of row. (48 stitches)
15 Slip 1 stitch and purl to the end.
16 Slip 1 stitch, knit 6, increase into the next stitch, (knit 7, increase into the next stitch). Repeat sequence in brackets to end of row. (54 stitches)
17 Slip 1 stitch and purl to the end.
18 Slip 1 stitch and knit to the end.
19 Slip 1 stitch and purl to the end.
20 Slip 1 stitch and knit to the end.
21 Slip 1 stitch and purl to the end.
22 Slip 1 stitch, purl 1, (pull a bead down the thread against the knitting, purl 4). Repeat sequence in brackets to end of the row. The beads just sit in the loop between two stitches on the front of the knitting.
23 Slip 1 stitch and purl to the end.
24 Slip 1 stitch, purl 3, (pull a bead down the thread against the knitting, purl 4). Repeat sequence in brackets to the last 2 stitches. Knit 2.
25 Slip 1 stitch and purl to the end.
26 Slip 1 stitch, purl 1, (pull a bead down the thread against the knitting, purl 4). Repeat sequence in brackets to the end.
27 Work a further 40 rows in stocking stitch, i.e., one row knit then one row purl, but don't forget to slip the first stitch of each row. During these 40 rows you will come to the end of the first skein of silk; join in a new one at the beginning of a row but before you do, thread

on the remaining size 6 beads ready for the next beaded band.

28 Repeat steps 23 to 27 to make another beaded band.

29 Repeat steps 17 to 21.

30 Slip 1 stitch, knit 6, knit 2 stitches together to make one, (knit 7, knit 2 together). Repeat sequence in brackets to end of row. (48 stitches)

31 Slip 1 stitch and purl to the end.

32 Slip 1 stitch, knit 5, knit 2 stitches together, (knit 6, knit 2 together). Repeat sequence in brackets to end of row. (42 stitches)

33 Slip 1 stitch and purl to the end.

34 Slip 1 stitch, knit 4, knit 2 stitches together, (knit 5, knit 2 together). Repeat sequence in brackets to end of row. (36 stitches)

35 Slip 1 stitch and purl to the end.

36 Slip 1 stitch, knit 3, knit 2 stitches together, (knit 4, knit 2 together). Repeat sequence in brackets to end of row. (30 stitches)

37 Slip 1 stitch and purl to the end.

38 Slip 1 stitch, knit 2, knit 2 stitches together, (knit 3, knit 2 together). Repeat sequence in brackets to end of row. (24 stitches)

39 Slip 1 stitch and purl to the end.

40 Slip 1 stitch, knit 1, knit 2 stitches together, (knit 2, knit 2 together). Repeat sequence in brackets to end of row. (18 stitches)

41 Slip 1 stitch and purl to the end.

42 Slip 1 stitch, knit 2 stitches together, (knit 1, knit 2 together). Repeat sequence in brackets to end of row. (12 stitches)

43 Slip 1 stitch and purl to the end.

44 Knit 2 together six times. Cut the thread leaving a tail of about 30cm (12in), thread the end through all the six remaining stitches and pull them up together.

Making up

1 Make a tassel by taking eight 85cm (33in) lengths of the thinner thread and fold in half and half again. Take another length, fold as before and twist to make a short cord but before you fold in half to make the cord, loop it around the mid point of the tassel strands so the tassel lies in the loop and then allow it to twist to make a cord for the tassel. Take a 30cm (12in) length and thread both ends into a tapestry needle leaving a loop at the bottom. Fold the tassel at the cord and make a loop around it by laying the doubled threads around the neck of the tassel 1cm (⅜in) from the top and passing the needle through the loop at the end. Wind tightly around a few times, stitch through the windings and leave the end within the tassel. Trim ends to 4cm (1½in). Repeat for the second tassel.

2 Tuck the cord of a tassel into the end of the knitting, fold right sides together and sew the seam to just past the beaded band on each end.

3 Work buttonhole stitch all around a plastic ring (see pictures, right), catching in the end and working over it when you get about two-thirds round. Finish the end neatly. Thread a beading needle with beading thread and, working backwards and forwards through the coil of the buttonhole stitch, attach a seed bead to either side as you work around the circle. Work around again, stitching beads evenly to the outside of the coil. Repeat for the second ring.

4 To line the purse make a tube of lining to fit, gather up both ends, slip it inside the purse, turn the edge in and slipstitch it around the opening. To finish, slip both beaded rings on to the purse.

Tip Plastic rings usually have a nasty catchy bit on them. Remove this by filing with an emery board before you start to cover with silk.

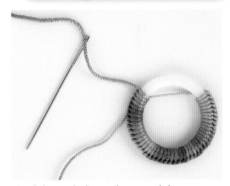

Work buttonhole stitch around the ring

Attach seed beads either side of the ring

Pearly Queen Bag

There was a time when every self-respecting shirt had a set of mother-of-pearl buttons but now we have plastic instead – what progress! The Pearly Kings and Queens of old London knew a thing or two; those wonderful suits they wore had so many buttons sewn on that the original fabric was almost invisible. Now such beautiful buttons are appreciated again, and this little bag is a way of displaying a collection. Old lace is much nicer than modern versions, and the creamy colour will be much more in harmony with the shell buttons. Search antique shops and sales as many have a basket of old lace tucked away and it is often only a few coins for a bundle. I have used a piece of hand-dyed silk velvet to make my bag and an old-fashioned clasp. See Suppliers for details of materials.

1 Trace the actual size template on page 116 and cut this out to make a paper pattern. Cut two pieces in velvet and two pieces in lining fabric.

2 Make two rows of gathering stitches on each of the four pieces as marked on the pattern but do not pull the gathers up yet.

3 Take the piece of velvet that will be the front of the bag and lay your lace and buttons on it to make a pleasing arrangement (see the useful Tip on page 40 about taking a picture of your composition). The lace will look better at an angle rather than straight across but it will depend on the particular piece you have. Try to find some with a pretty edge. Keep the lace below the gathered edge as this will be stitched into the metal edge of the clasp and the lace would make it too thick.

4 Stitch around the edge of the lace and velvet and trim the lace to the same shape as the velvet. Sew the top edge of the lace to the velvet – it will probably be best to do this by hand so the stitches do not show.

5 Attach all the buttons in the right places using matching sewing thread.

Making up

1 Place the bag front and back right sides together and sew a seam from one end of the gathers to the other around the bottom edge. Do the same with the two pieces of lining fabric. Now turn the bag right side out and slip the lining bag inside.

2 Open the clasp and work with one side first. Gather the bag and the lining the same amount using both rows of stitching. You are going to turn in the edges of the velvet and the lining on the area between the two rows of gathering and then stitch the whole lot to the clasp. Having two rows of gathering helps because it gives a flat area to work on. As you cannot pin through the metal edge it's a bit tricky, but do it bit by bit and it's not as difficult as it first seems. You'll find that it looks better if there are more gathers in the centre top rather than down the sides. Use backstitch through the holes of the clasp and strong thread. Repeat for the other side.

3 Cut a strip of velvet 7 x 40cm (2¾ x 16in) for the handle. Fold it in half lengthways right sides together, sew a seam along the length and turn right side out (see the Tip on page 37). Turn in the ends and slipstitch them. Sew buttons all along the length of this strip and then attach one end to each of the loops on the clasp to finish your bag.

Farmyard Tote

Every little girl loves a bag to keep treasures in. I made lots of bags for my daughters when they were tiny and I can still see the chubby little hands holding the handles a bit too tight. This bag is sure to please, especially if you use the funny little charms (I never thought a worm could be charming!). It would be perfect as an Easter present filled with shiny Easter eggs. It is very easy to stitch – simply lay the canvas over the drawing and trace straight on to the threads, then fill the shapes with the wool or stranded cotton colours in simple stitches. I have listed the colours I used but you could use threads you already have to make your own version. As the picture is drawn on to the canvas, don't worry about making yours exactly the same as mine; it will vary a little and that will be its charm.

Finished bag size, excluding handles: 21.5 x 23.5cm (8½ x 9¼in)

Tip If the pen you use isn't waterproof it is likely to bleed colour on to your embroidery when you stretch it. To be sure the ink is waterproof, scribble on a scrap of canvas and then rub it with a piece of wet tissue; if no colour comes off it is safe to use.

1 Lay the canvas over the drawing on page 76 and trace it on to the canvas using a waterproof felt-tip pen. You could photocopy the drawing and work from that rather than mark your book.

2 The bag features tent stitch, rice stitch, cross stitch, satin stitch, bullion knots, velvet stitch and gobelin filling stitch – see Stitches page 108. All the stitching in stranded cotton (floss) is worked using all six strands of thread.

Cow and calf
Work in tent stitch in stranded cotton. Bodies in very dark brown and ecru. Noses and horns in soft brown. Nostrils and udders in pink. The end of the cow's tail has three velvet stitches in ecru and the calf's ears are worked in straight stitches to shape.

Pig
All in tent stitch in stranded cotton. Spots and ears in grey. Nose in light terracotta. Eye in soft brown. Tail in grey straight stitches to shape. Body and head in pig pink.

Hen and chick
Mostly in tent stitch in stranded cotton. Hen in gold with an eye in soft brown and three stitches in dark terracotta between the head and body. Chick in light gold with an eye in soft brown. Feet and beaks are straight stitches of soft brown in stranded cotton. Wings, tails and head feathers are all worked in stranded cotton bullion knots – dark terracotta for the hen and pink for the chick.

Sheep
Faces in tent stitch in pink stranded cotton. Feet in grey tent stitch in stranded cotton and ears of straight stitch, to shape. Bodies in velvet stitch in one strand of cream crewel wool.

Flowers and grass
All in straight stitches in stranded cotton to fill the shape. Leaves and grass in dark green. Flower petals in gold. Flower centres in light terracotta tent stitch under a cluster of French knots.

Stones and fence
Stones in tent stitch using one strand each of light fawn and dark fawn crewel wool. Fence in gobelin filling over four canvas threads using one strand each of light fawn and dark fawn crewel wool.

House

Work the roof in three strands of crewel wool in mid fawn gobelin filling stitch over four canvas threads. Window frame and door in dark blue stranded cotton in satin stitch; work the lower part of the door in rows of diagonal satin stitch over two canvas threads. Windows in tent stitch in three strands each of grey and light blue stranded cotton together in the needle. Window box and doorstep in two strands of dark fawn satin stitch in crewel wool. Now work the flowers in the window box with two strands of crewel wool in mid green tent stitch with French knots scattered in red and gold stranded cotton. The bricks are in rows of satin stitch over two canvas threads alternating two stitches in light terracotta with two in dark terracotta stranded cotton. Chimney pots in tent stitch in dark terracotta stranded cotton.

Tree

Trunk in stranded cotton in straight stitches to fill the shape, with French knots on top in light brown. Work leaves in cross stitch over two canvas threads using one strand each of mid green and dark green crewel wool.

Hill

Using bright green stranded cotton work diagonal rows over one canvas thread and then over two; carry on stitching diagonally alternating a long stitch with a short stitch. When you work the following row work a short stitch against a long one on the first row, then carry on working diagonally until you have filled the shape. Work around the sheep, filling any gaps with single stitches. The hill also shows through to the left of the house.

Bushes

The two on the hill and the one at the base of the tree are in tent stitch in two strands of mid green crewel wool with a few French knots in the same colour scattered over the surface.

Cloud and sky

Work the cloud in rice stitch in two strands of cream crewel wool. Fill in with a few cross stitches to create the shape right. Work the sky in three strands each of blue and light blue stranded cotton together in gobelin filling stitch worked horizontally over two canvas threads.

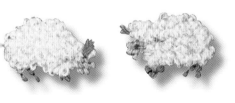

Foreground

Work in one strand each of yellow and light green crewel wool together in gobelin filling stitch worked over two canvas threads.

Making up

1 Stretch the canvas piece to bring it back to square (see page 106). Trim the bare canvas edges to 1.25cm (½in).

2 Cut two pieces of lining 25 x 27cm (10 x 10½in). From the linen cut:
   two pieces 6 x 18cm (2½ x 7in) for side panels;
   two pieces 6 x 27cm (2½ x 10½in) for top and bottom panels;
   one piece 25 x 27cm (10 x 10½in) for the back;
   two pieces 8 x 35cm (3¼ x 14in) for handles.

3 Sew a side panel to each side of the embroidery by laying the panel right sides together with the embroidery and stitching as close to the edge as you can. Sew the top and bottom panels to the embroidery as for the side panels.

4 If using charms, sew them on where you like, using matching thread.

5 Place the front right sides together with the back, stitch the sides and bottom and turn right sides out.

6 Fold the handles in half lengthwise, sew the seam and turn right side out. Pin the handles to the top edge of the bag.

7 Sew the side seams of the lining. Place the lining over the bag, right sides together, and pin in place around the top edge. Sew the seam of the top edge, attaching the handles as you do so. Pull the lining up from the bag and turn the bottom edges in and topstitch the seam. Push the lining down inside the bag to finish.

Farmyard Tote – thread colours used

DMC stranded cotton		Appletons crewel wool	
ecru		357	dk green
349	red	542	lt green
355	lt terracotta	545	mid green
356	dk terracotta	693	yellow
414	grey	903	mid fawn
470	bright green	904	dk fawn
676	lt gold	952	lt fawn
758	pink	992	cream
783	gold		
799	blue		
800	lt blue		
839	soft brown		
930	dk blue		
937	dk green		
3021	lt brown		
3371	vy dk brown		
3773	pig pink		

Crazy Patchwork Handbag

This bright bag was inspired by Victorian crazy patchwork, which was created from scraps of fabric not cut to regular shapes but just pieced together as they were. Joins were then hand stitched over with feather stitch, usually in yellow silk. I started with random shapes and discovered that I could make a lovely three-dimensional bag by stitching squares together on point. Although the shapes became very regular, the feather stitching gives this bag an old-fashioned feel on a new shape. I have used five shades of flame-coloured silk dupion but the choice is yours. The feather stitch is worked in a shiny rayon space-dyed thread, and I added four antique buttons where the handles join the bag. The handles are made from tubes of silk, ruched up by threading piping cord through them.

Finished bag size, excluding handles: 16 x 19cm (6¼ x 7½in)

Tip The seaming to make this bag is actually very easy once you see it, but if you have trouble working it out draw the diagram on a piece of paper and then cut it out. Join the seams together with staples or pins to make a model of the bag and see how the seaming works.

1 The silk dupion needs stiffening to hold the shape of the bag and it's easier to iron the stiffening on to the back of the pieces of silk before you cut the squares. Once you have enough stiffened silk cut out twenty-two 8 x 8cm (3¼ x 3¼in) squares. I suggest you draw the squares with a faint pencil line on the stiffened side of the silk and then cut carefully along the lines. It is important that the squares are cut carefully and accurately so they fit together perfectly. The ironed-on stiffening also stops the silk fraying at the edges.

2 Arrange the squares as in the diagram opposite, so no two like squares are next to each other and so that seams will not bring like squares together. The lines marked with two yellow dashes will come together, as will the ones marked with three red dashes.

3 Sew the squares together a line at a time starting with 1 and 2 at the top. Then sew 3, 4, 5 and 6 together and so on, placing the strips of stitched squares back in their correct places before picking up the next row. Once all the strips in one direction are joined press all the seams open.

4 Machine sew the strips together to make one piece. Take two strips of squares and stitch them together matching seams very carefully. Add strip after strip until you have made a flat piece like the diagram and then press all the seams open.

Making up

1 Lay the flat piece of patchwork on the lining fabric and using the patchwork as a pattern cut out a piece the same shape.

2 Work feather stitch (see page 109) with one strand of space-dyed thread over all the completed seams of the patchwork.

3 To seam up the sides of the bag and give it shape, sew the squares together marked by the arrows on the diagram. Bring the right sides together so that the seams are on the inside of the bag. There are four of these short seams.

4 Now sew the side seams. Join the squares marked with two dashes together and then carry on stitching the ones marked with three dashes. Work feather stitch over all the seams that do not already have it.

5 Cut two pieces of silk 5 x 70cm (2 x 27½in) to make the handles. Fold them in half lengthwise, sew a seam along the length and then turn the tube right sides out. Cut the piece of piping in half to make two 30cm (12in)

lengths. Thread a length of piping cord through each handle, gather the silk to fit the length of the cord and secure the ends.

6 Turn over the edges of the top four squares of the bag (two on each side) and attach the ends of the handles.

7 Take the piece of silk you cut to make a lining and seam it in the same way as the bag. Tuck it inside the bag, turn the top edges in and slipstitch them down around the top edge, hiding the edges of the handles as you do so.

8 To finish, sew buttons to the bottom of the handles as a trimming or use beads, old brooches or clusters of sequins.

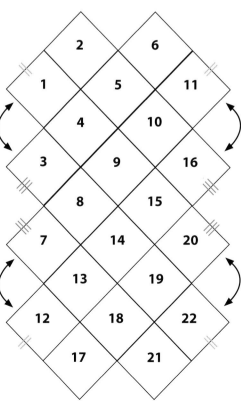

Layout of the patchwork squares – the squares marked with three red dashes will meet when seamed; the squares marked with two yellow dashes will meet when seamed.

Tassel Purse

This design is not for the faint-hearted as it is a bit complicated but the effect is stunning and it's very interesting to work – so if you like a bit of a challenge this is the one for you. The combination of matte wool and lustrous stranded cotton creates contrast. I have made tassels with a three-dimensional, humbug-shaped piece and then used another without the tassel to make a fat button. The back and the front of the bag are slightly different because the bargello panel is on the top on one side and the bottom on the other. Stitches used in the bag are tent stitch, long-legged cross stitch, French knots, satin stitch and Rhodes stitch – see page 108 for working. The colours I've used are deep and rich but the purse would also look wonderful in a range of pastel shades.

*Finished bag size, excluding strap
and tassels:
10 x 12cm (4 x 4¾in)*

1 Prepare the canvas for work (see page 106) and follow the charts on page 86. The bargello (wave pattern) chart is shown separately because its long straight stitches are worked *in between* the horizontal canvas threads, whereas the stitches of the main pattern are worked *over* both horizontal and vertical threads. The colours of the crewel wool are marked with a dot. Use two strands of crewel wool and all six strands of stranded cotton throughout.

2 Work the large chart first and then fill in the two empty areas with the bargello pattern. In the main pattern, the squares with a diamond shape inset in them are worked in tent stitch (see picture below). I have faced all the stitches towards the four corners of the square so work each quarter of the square separately. Look at the picture to see the stitches of the outer row of each of these squares in gold stranded cotton, showing the direction change.

3 Work the chequered border to these squares in blocks of satin stitch, the lines on the squares show the direction of the stitches. Work a single gold Rhodes stitch in the centre of the squares. Rows of dark red long-legged cross stitch divide the squares from the areas to be worked in bargello.

4 A row of navy long-legged cross stitch surrounds the central panel. To either side beyond the central panel work the following:
• Two rows of satin stitch squares, gold alternating with orange and dark red alternating with red stranded cotton, the lines indicate the stitch direction. These squares have peacock blue and mauve French knots alternating at the corners all the way up the strip.
• One row of mauve tent stitch in stranded cotton.
• One row of long-legged cross stitch in red crewel wool.
• One row of peacock blue tent stitch in stranded cotton.
• Diagonal satin stitch in crewel wool, in chevrons of colour three stitches wide. Two rows of red alternating with gold and two rows of dark red alternating with navy. See picture opposite for details of these stitches.
• Finally, work a row of dark red tent stitch in stranded cotton.

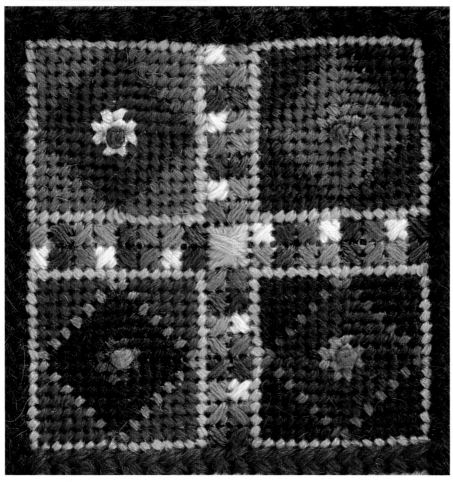

5 Work the bargello panels. The chart shows blocks of colour either two or four blocks long. Work these as long stitches either over four or two vertical canvas threads. Work a row of long-legged cross stitch in dark red crewel wool along both short sides of the panel. These will be the top edges of the bag.

6 The two little charted squares are for the tassels and button. Work these, two canvas threads apart, three times on the three small pieces of canvas.

Making up

1 Stretch all the canvas pieces to bring them back to square (see page 106).

2 Use 85cm (33in) lengths of crewel wool to make two tassels and a button. Take four lengths of dark red and cut these four threads in half. Take one of these sets and twist them until they double back to make a cord. Fold in half and knot to make a short length of cord and set aside. Take two threads of each colour, fold in half and in half again. Take the other set of dark red threads and twist as before but before you fold in half to make the cord, loop it around the mid point of the tassel strands so the tassel lies in the loop and then allow it to twist to make a cord for the tassel. Now take one thread of dark red and thread both ends in your needle leaving a loop at the bottom. Fold the tassel at the cord and make a loop around it by laying the doubled thread around the tassel neck 1cm (⅜in) from the top and then pass the needle through the loop at the end. Wind tightly around a few times and finish off by going through the windings and leaving an end hanging within the tassel threads. Trim the tassel ends to 4cm (1½in). Make two tassels and three cords in this way.

3 Make two more cords for the tie around the button. Take four strands of dark red wool and twist and fold to make a cord, knotting the ends together.

4 Trim the tassel embroideries to within 1cm (⅜in) of the embroidery and clip corners. Fold in all edges leaving a canvas thread exposed. Fold the oblong in half along the empty canvas threads. Work long-legged cross stitch in dark red wool down these empty threads. Carry on at the corner, making a seam by taking one canvas thread from each folded-over edge, tucking in one end of a tassel cord halfway along. Continue up the third side and finish at the top. Fold the open top edge in the opposite way to make the three-dimensional shape, bringing the ends of the two rows of long-legged cross stitch together at the middle of the next seam. As you join this final seam tuck in a cord and before completing the seam stuff the shape with polyester stuffing. Repeat for the other tassel and make a third one with just a cord for the button.

Tip You could very easily add a useful pocket to the inside of this bag on one of the sides – see page 107 for instructions.

5 Trim the bare canvas edges to 1.25cm (½in) on the large embroidery and use this as a pattern to cut out a lining the same size. Turn in the long sides leaving one canvas thread exposed. Fold the bag right sides together and join the sides with long-legged cross stitch, working one canvas thread from each side to make a seam. Tuck the cord from a tassel into these seams as you reach the bottom edge of the bag.

6 Sew the cord from the button on to one side in the centre of the top of the bag and the two ties to the other.

7 To make the twisted cord for the handle, take four 200cm (80in) lengths of stranded cotton in blue, red, gold and mauve. Take the blue thread and twist in the same direction as it is already twisted, until the thread begins to double back on itself. Fold in half and let go of the centre point gradually, holding the two ends together. Knot the ends together. Take the red length and repeat the above, except that before you fold in half and allow it to twist, thread the twisted length through the looped end of the blue cord and then fold with the first cord in the looped end of the second cord. The cord length is now double, one half of each colour. Twist again and fold to make a cord of blue and red. Repeat with the gold and mauve threads for a second cord but thread the second through the loop of the first to make a cord blue/red at one end and gold/mauve at the other. Twist and fold again to finish the multicoloured cord. Knot the ends together each time you twist or your cords will unravel. Sew one end of the cord to the top of the bag at each side.

8 Sew up the sides of the lining. Tuck it inside the bag and turn the top edge over and slipstitch in place to finish you bag.

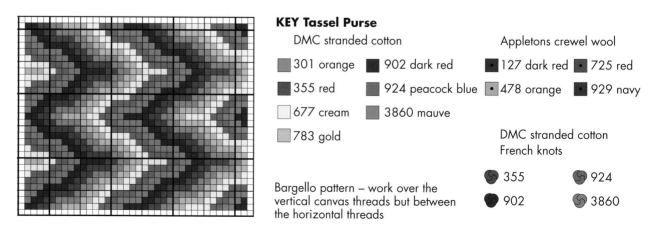

KEY Tassel Purse

DMC stranded cotton

- 301 orange
- 902 dark red
- 355 red
- 924 peacock blue
- 677 cream
- 3860 mauve
- 783 gold

Bargello pattern – work over the vertical canvas threads but between the horizontal threads

Appletons crewel wool

- 127 dark red
- 725 red
- 478 orange
- 929 navy

DMC stranded cotton French knots

- 355
- 924
- 902
- 3860

Main purse pattern

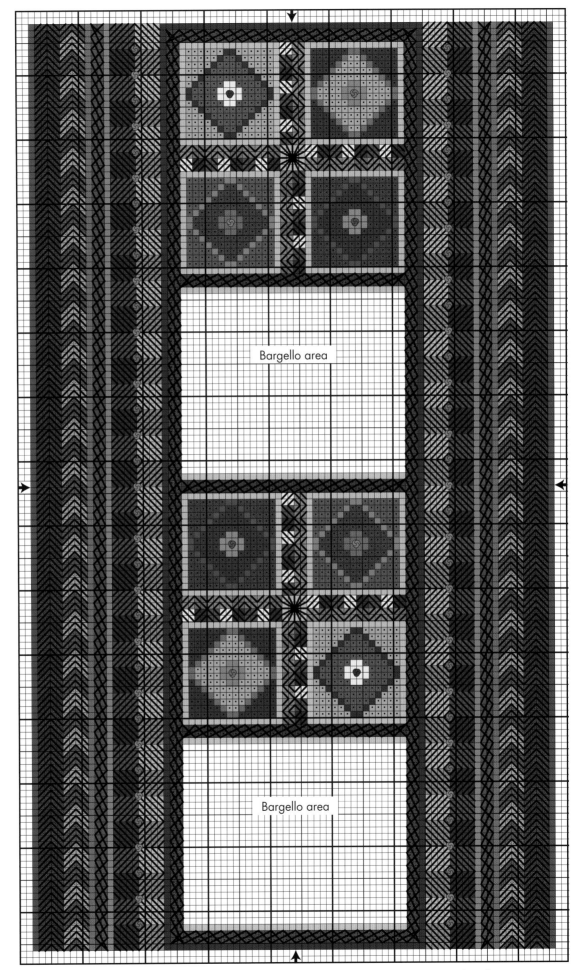

Bargello area

Bargello area

Tassel patterns

Denim Rose Phone Bag

I don't really subscribe to the idea that you should have to carry a mobile phone around with you all the time but there are some calls that you will need when you are out and about. This little neck purse saves all that embarrassing rummaging around in a large handbag while the ring tone gets ever louder. The pretty rose motif is worked in seed beads in lovely shades of pink and green while the denim is hearty enough to protect the phone. I have used mixed strands of dark and light blue and pink to go with the faded denim. If you have a really small phone, work just to the inner pink border. I have used the leg from an old well-worn and washed pair of jeans but you will find denim in most fabric shops.

Finished bag size, excluding strap: 14 x 9.5cm (5½ x 3¾in)

1 Prepare the canvas for work (see page 106) and follow the chart opposite.

2 Begin at the top of the beaded area on the chart and work a row from left to right and then a second row from right to left, attaching the beads with beading thread and half cross stitch (see page 113). Usually when working beading from a chart you work in a single colour of thread with the design going on one bead at a time in different colours, so there is no need to work areas of colour. By working rows you will keep a more even tension on the beading thread and so the beads will sit well.

3 Using two strands of dark pink and two of light pink stranded cotton (floss) together in the needle work the borders in cross stitch. Fill in the background in cross stitch using two strands of dark blue and two of light blue together in the needle.

Making up

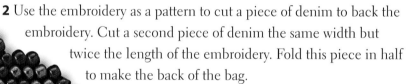

1 Stretch the canvas to bring it back to square (see page 106). However carefully you have stitched it will still have distorted a little and the stretching process will restore the shape and even up your tension. Trim the bare canvas edge to 1.25cm (½in).

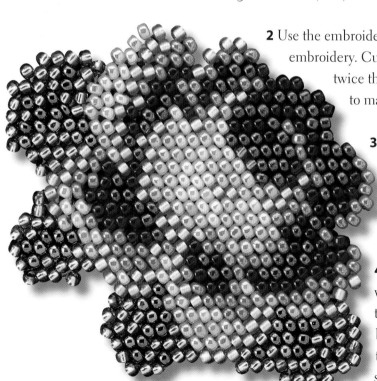

2 Use the embroidery as a pattern to cut a piece of denim to back the embroidery. Cut a second piece of denim the same width but twice the length of the embroidery. Fold this piece in half to make the back of the bag.

3 Place the embroidery right sides together with its backing piece and sew a seam across the top edge. Trim and turn right sides out. Place the front and back of the bag together and sew around the three edges, seam on the outside.

4 Cut a strip of denim for binding 4cm (1¾in) wide and 10cm (4in) long. Sew this, right sides together, along the bottom edge of the bag on the back side. Trim the seam to 7mm (¼in) and turn the binding to the right side, turn it under and top stitch it down. Trim the excess at each end.

5 The strap on my bag measures 122cm (48in) from one point at the bottom of the bag to the other but you may want to alter this to suit you. Cut enough 4cm (1¾in) wide strips to make a handle as long as you require and join them if necessary. You will probably be able to make this all in one piece if you are using new fabric but will need to add a join if you've used old jeans.

6 Sew the ends of the strip to the back sides of the bag. Turn the binding to the front, trim the seam, turn the edge in and pin it down. Pin the edges of the strap in and then you will be able to top stitch up one side, all around the strap and down the other side. Turn the ends in as you do this; if your denim is very thick leave ends below the level of the bottom of the bag so that the edge doesn't become too thick to sew through.

Tip You could add a long pocket to the back of this bag to hold a pair of spectacles. Then you will have your specs to hand to see who it is interrupting before you answer! See page 107 for basic instructions on adding a pocket.

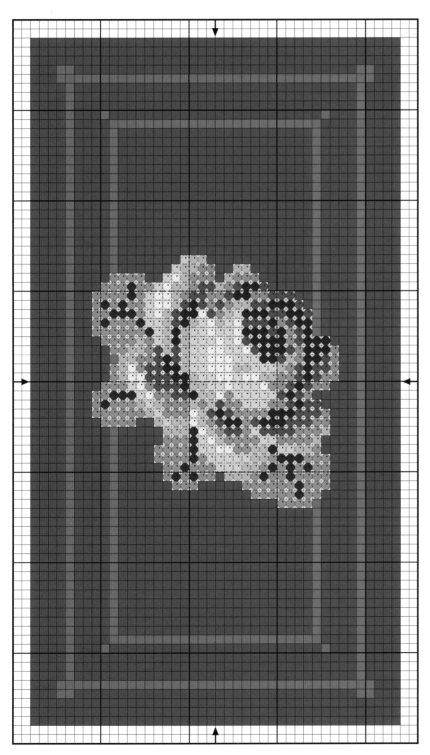

KEY Denim Rose Phone Bag

Mill Hill seed beads (1 packet each)

- ● 03033
- ● 00367
- ● 00968
- ● 03057
- ● 02004
- ○ 02003
- ● 03035
- ● 03055
- ● 03026

DMC stranded cotton (1 skein each)

930 + 931
(2 strands of each together in needle)

3721 + 3722
(2 strands of each together in needle)

Pansy Amulet Purses

The two charming amulet purses in this chapter are worked in the same collection of colours. The triangular one (shown right) is made from a square with two adjacent sides folded in and joined to give a shape like those little bags that we used to be able to buy filled with loose sweets. A pair of small needlework scissors fits perfectly into the pointy bag and you can also keep a few needles in the lid. It has a sweet little pansy flower embroidered in a heart shape and surrounded by rows of carefully counted stitches. The little square purse (shown on page 97) is simpler to make but is just as pretty and will hold a few coins or some little treasure dear to a girl's heart. Both purses are trimmed with multicoloured tassels and cords made out of the stranded cotton they are stitched in.

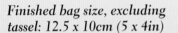

YOU WILL NEED

25 x 25cm (10 x 10in)
18-count interlock canvas

Size 22 tapestry needle

DMC stranded cotton (floss)
as listed in chart key

15 x 15cm (6 x 6in) silk
for lining

One decorative button

*Finished bag size, excluding
tassel: 12.5 x 10cm (5 x 4in)*

Triangular Pansy Purse

1 Prepare the canvas for work (see page 106) and follow the chart on page 98. Use all six strands of stranded cotton (floss) for all the stitching. Refer to Stitches (page 108 onwards) for working all the stitches used.

2 Work the larger heart shape in dark pink tent stitch in the centre of the canvas. Then work the three mid pink Rhodes stitches within the heart.

3 Lay the canvas over the pansy template, far right, and draw a pencil outline on the canvas. Stitching the heart first allows you to place the pansy in the right place, which is easier than stitching the heart around the flower.

4 Using light gold work a row of long and short stitch along the outer edge of the bottom three petals, working from the outside in and overlapping stitches towards the centre of the flower to make them radiate outwards. Make the stitches longer than you feel you should as they will be shortened by the next row. Work the next row in dark gold, this time from the inside out, splitting the threads of the previous stitches to blend the colours. Work the top two petals in dark and light mauve. Fill the flower centre with a tight cluster of dark pink French knots. Work the leaves in light green in long and short stitch.

5 Fill all the background of the heart with alternating long and short stitches in light pink. Begin working as shown on the chart and carry on in diagonal rows making a long stitch next to a short one on the last row. Allow the flower to break into the stitches, making short stitches to fill any gaps.

6 Work all the rows of long-legged cross stitch between the bands of different stitches and then go on to work all the bands of different stitches.

7 Work the second small heart shape at the corner of the square and fill it with Rhodes stitches and tent stitch as shown. Then work the rows of tent stitch and satin stitch waves across the square. Finish the embroidery by working the rows of long-legged cross stitch that surround the whole piece.

Making up

1 Stretch the canvas piece to bring it back to square (see page 106). Trim the bare canvas edges to 1.25cm (½in). Use this embroidered piece as a pattern to cut out the same square in lining.

2 Make one tassel and a cord as described overleaf.

3 Fold in the canvas edges on the two sides that have a double row of long-legged cross stitch leaving one thread of canvas exposed. Work dark pink long-legged cross stitch on these exposed threads taking one canvas thread from each side to make a join. When you reach the bottom point tuck the little cord from the tassel in as you finish the stitching. Stitch one end of the cord to either side of the triangular purse just inside the top.

4 Make a lining to fit by sewing two sides together. Push the lining into the bag, turn the edges over and slipstitch in place around the top edge.

5 To finish, turn the flap over and make a buttonhole loop (see page 108) on the point of it. Stitch on a button in the right place for the loop.

Pansy template (actual size)

Square Purse

1 Prepare the canvas for work (see page 106) and follow the chart on page 99. Use all six strands of stranded cotton (floss) for all the stitching.

2 Fold the canvas in half across the shortest length, to mark the fold that will be the purse bottom (the line between the two squares of stitching on chart).

3 Work all the rows of long-legged cross stitch between the bands of different stitches, using the colours given in the chart key.

4 Work all the bands of different stitches on both squares and then go on to surround both squares with alternating satin stitch bands of dark mauve and mid pink as on the chart.

5 Work a row of dark pink long-legged cross stitch at the top and bottom – this will become the two top edges of the purse when it is folded.

Making up

1 Stretch the canvas piece to bring it back to square (see page 106). Trim the bare canvas edges to 1.25cm (½in). Use the embroidery as a pattern to cut out the same shape in lining.

2 Make a twisted cord as follows. Take four 200cm (80in) lengths of dark pink, dark gold, dark green and dark mauve. Take the pink threads and twist in the same direction as they are already slightly twisted (i.e., you are adding to this twist and

Square Purse
YOU WILL NEED

15 x 20cm (6 x 8in) 18-count interlock canvas

Size 22 tapestry needle

DMC stranded cotton (floss) as listed in chart key

10 x 20cm (4 x 8in) silk lining

Finished bag size, excluding strap/tassels: 6.5cm (2½in) square

not untwisting it). Twist until the thread begins to double back on itself when you release the tension slightly. Fold in half and let go of the centre point gradually, holding the two ends together. Knot the ends together. Take the green length and repeat the above, except that before you fold it in half and allow to twist, thread the twisted length through the looped end of the pink cord and then fold with the first cord in the looped end of the second cord. You will have doubled the length of the cord, one half of each colour. Twist again and fold to make a cord of green and pink. Repeat with the gold and mauve threads to make a second cord but thread the second through the loop of the first to make a cord pink/green at one end and gold/mauve at the other. Twist and fold one final time to make the finished multicoloured cord. Every time you twist and fold you must knot the ends together or your cords will simply untwist.

3 Make a tassel as follows. Take one 80cm (31½in) length of each colour and two of dark mauve (ten strands in total), fold them in half once and then fold in half again. Take a further length of dark mauve and cut it in half. Take one of these pieces, fold it double and twist it tightly, loop it around the mid point of the tassel strands so that the tassel lies in the loop and then allow it to twist to make a cord for the tassel. Thread both ends of the other half length of dark mauve in your needle, fold the tassel at the cord and make a loop around it by laying the double thread around the neck of the tassel about 1.25cm (½in) from the top, and then pass the needle through the loop at the end of the thread. Wind tightly around a few times and finish off by stitching through the windings and leaving an end hanging amongst the tassel threads. If you want to add the macramé type trim to the tassel, pull eight dark mauve threads to the surface of the tassel and knot four pairs together around the tassel about 7mm (¼in) below the neck – use a needle in the knot to move it to the correct position. Now make a second row of knots about 7mm (¼in) below the first set, tying in pairs one from each of the first knots. Trim the ends of the tassel to about 5cm (2in) and then comb out the strands of the stranded cotton with your needle to separate them. Make a second tassel in the same way.

4 Fold in the canvas edges leaving one thread of canvas exposed on the sides of the embroidery. Fold the purse in half and, starting at the top edge join one side. Work this seam from the outside with dark pink long-legged cross stitch by taking one canvas thread from each folded-over edge. Work down the first side and tuck the cord of one of the tassels into the seam at the very bottom. Then work across the bottom of the purse on the two canvas threads that lie between the two sides of the purse, tuck the second tassel into the seam and then up the other side. Attach the cord to either side of the top of the purse to finish. To make a lining, refer to step 4 of the triangular purse.

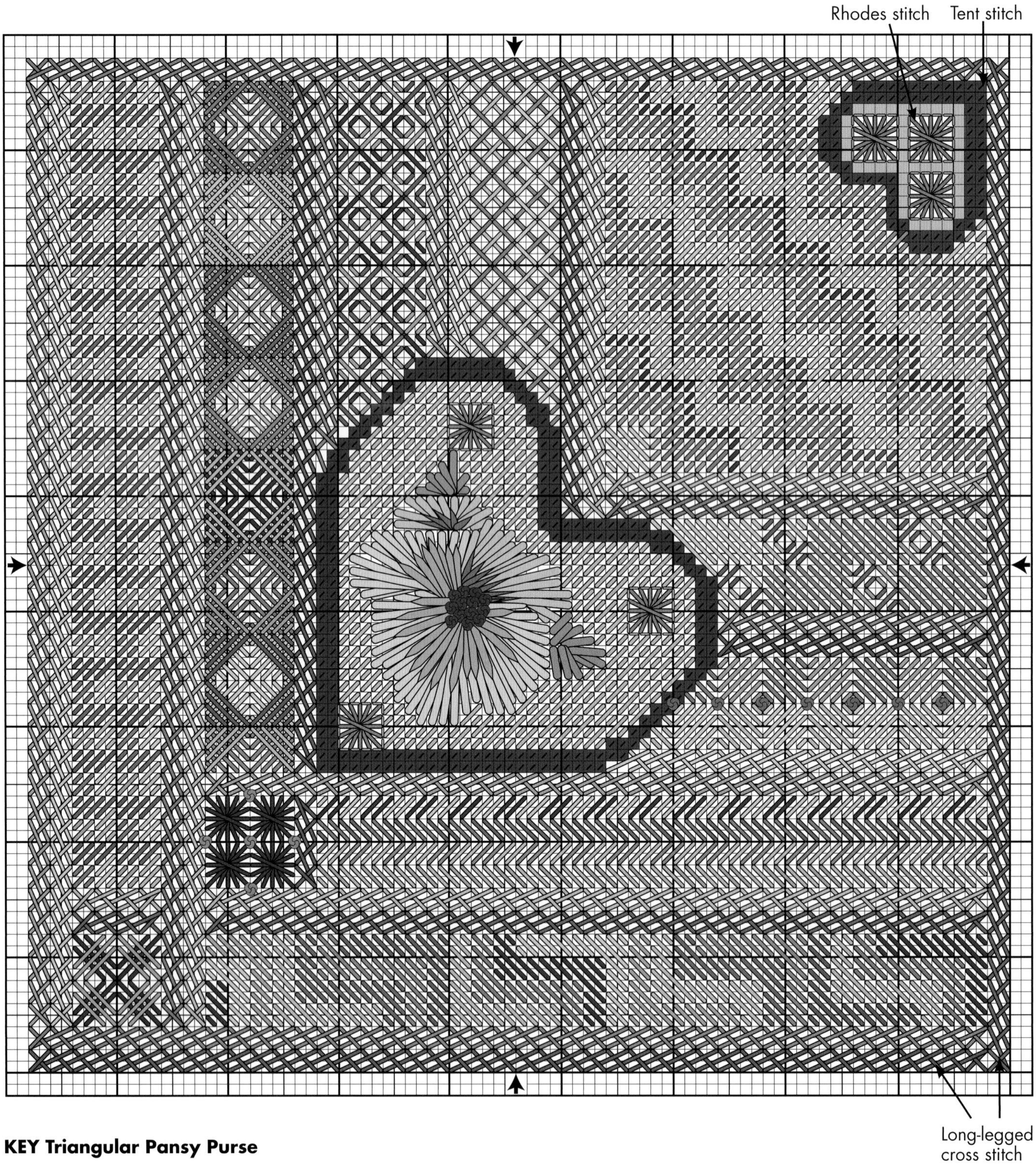

Rhodes stitch   Tent stitch

Long-legged
cross stitch

KEY Triangular Pansy Purse

DMC stranded cotton
(2 skeins of each colour)

French Knots

	221 dark pink		676 light gold		3012 light green		221
	223 mid pink		783 dark gold		3042 light mauve		3012
	224 light pink		3011 dark green		3740 dark mauve		3740

DMC stranded cotton

■ 221 dark pink

■ 223 mid pink

□ 224 light pink

□ 676 light gold

▨ 783 dark gold

▨ 3011 dark green

▨ 3012 light green

□ 3042 light mauve

■ 3740 dark mauve

Long-legged
cross stitch

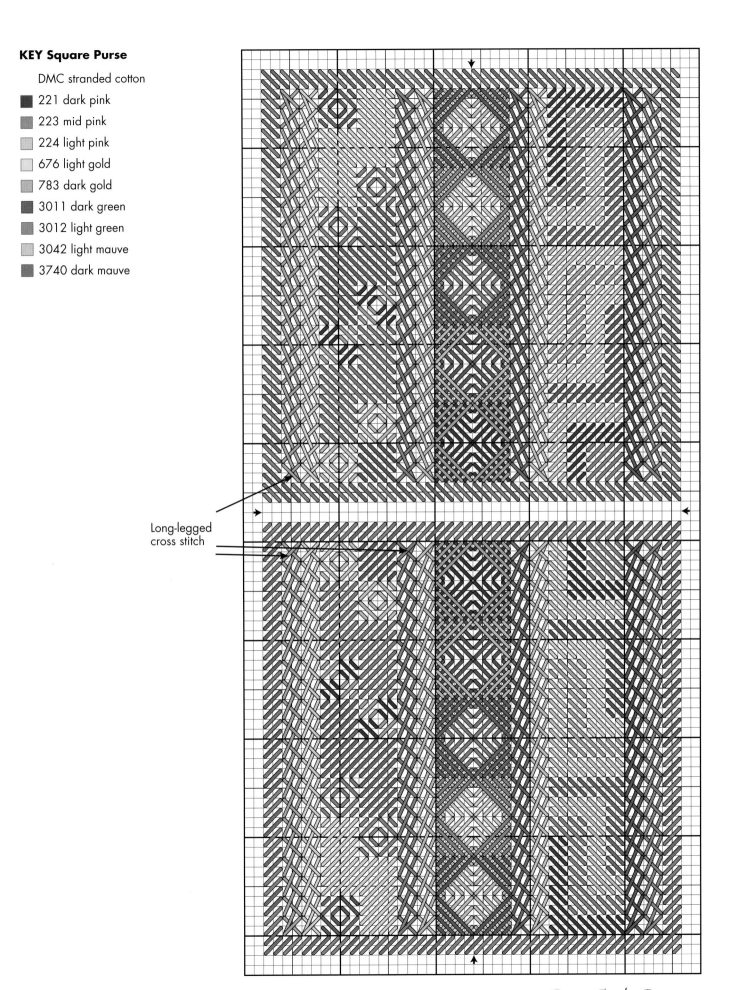

Venetian Knitted Pouch

To me, this beaded knitted pouch has a medieval feel to it but perhaps that's because it looks a little like one of those fearful weapons that knights used to hit each other with. I enjoy knitting because it fascinates me that you are able to produce a fabric from a single strand, and the repetitive action is somehow very soothing. This bag is made on a circular needle so you just keep going round and round from the outside with a simple knit stitch. The lovely Venetian glass beads are all irregular with knobbly spots on them and the hard surface of the glass contrasts well with the woolly bag. Twisted cords have knotted and beaded ends to pull the bag closed. I have used a beautiful yarn with a hand-dyed, hand-spun look to it but you could choose a different colour.

The addition of beads to the ends of the cords helps to keep the bag closed.

I have given the tension for the wool and needles I used but if you use a thinner or thicker wool your bag may end up bigger or smaller than mine.

1 Cast on 64 stitches.

2 Knit two rounds. As you start the first round you will be joining the two ends of the casting on together, so take care not to twist the stitches. Knot a loop of coloured thread and slip it over the needle to mark where the round starts; every time you reach this slip it from the left needle to the right and it will travel up the work with you – you will then always know where a new round starts.

3 Knit 2 together and then make one stitch by bringing the wool forwards over the needle from the back to the front. Repeat this all the way along the next round until you reach the marker again.

4 Knit the following round, knitting into all the slanting stitches that you made on the last round – these will make a row of holes in the knitting.

5 Knit another round.

6 As you knit the next round fold the cast-on edge up at the back of the knitting and as you push your needle through to knit a stitch pick up a loop of the cast-on edge as well and knit them both together. Do this for every stitch on the next round picking up the next loop from your cast-on edge each time. This makes a neat hem with a picot edge where the holes are folded over.

7 Knit a further 5 rounds.

8 Make a second row of holes all the way around for the cord to thread through. This time knit 2 stitches, make 1 and then knit 2 together. Repeat sequence all the way round.

9 Knit a further 6 rounds, knitting the loops in the same way as before for the first round.

10 Cut four 20cm (8in) lengths of crewel wool, thread them through one of the beads, twist these four strands tightly until they start to double back on themselves and then fold them in half with the bead in the middle and allow them to twist to make a cord. Knot the ends together. This gives you a bead on a stalk. Repeat for 47 others – you can do them all now or as you go along.

11 Knit into the first stitch of the next round and before you put the wool over the needle push it through the twisted cord of a bead. Now knit the stitch and the cord together to attach a bead on a stalk to your knitting. Make sure that the bead falls to the outside before you carry on. Knit 7 stitches. Repeat this sequence to the end of the round.

12 Knit 5 rounds.

13 Knit 4 stitches, attach a bead with the next stitch, knit 7 stitches. Repeat this sequence to the last 3 stitches of the round and knit them.

14 Knit 5 rounds.

15 Repeat steps 11 to 14 and then 11 again. You will now have 5 rows of beads on the knitting.

16 Knit 2 rounds.

17 Knit 6 stitches and knit the next 2 together. Repeat this sequence to the end of the round. (You will now have 56 stitches.)

18 Knit 5 stitches and knit the next 2 together. Repeat this sequence to the end of the round. (48 stitches)

19 Knit 4 stitches and knit the next 2 together. Repeat sequence to the end of the round. You will now have 40 stitches. At this point the round is getting a bit short for the circular needle and you may find it easier to change to double-pointed needles.

20 Knit 3 stitches and knit the next 2 together, adding a bead at the same time. Repeat this sequence to the end of the round. (32 stitches)

21 Knit 2 stitches and knit the next 2 together. Repeat this sequence to the end of the round. (24 stitches)

22 Knit 1 stitch and knit the next 2 together. Repeat this sequence to the end of the round. (16 stitches)

23 Knit 2 together eight times. (8 stitches)

24 Knit 2 together four times. Cut the wool, leaving enough of an end to finish off, thread the wool through the four stitches and pull tight to gather them.

25 Sew in the two ends of wool, one at the beginning of the knitting and one at the end.

26 Cut two lengths of wool 200cm (80in) long. Fold one length in half and twist it until it begins to double back on itself. Fold it in half and allow it to twist to make a cord. Knot the two ends together to prevent the cord unravelling. Make a second cord in the same way.

27 Thread one cord in and out of the holes all the way around the bag. Fold the other cord in half and thread one end in and out from one of the holes where the first cord comes out, and then the other end the other way. You will have a pair of ends hanging out each side of the bag. Tie these cords together 5cm (2in) from the ends. Separate out the threads of the resulting tassels – there will be eight strands in each. Thread beads on to four of these and tie a knot to keep them on. Trim the other ends off nearly down to the knot to finish.

Tip You could add a lining to this bag to stop little bits and pieces from poking through the knitting. Use a fine fabric that doesn't alter the softness of the bag. Make a tube the same diameter as the bag and gather up one end. Tuck it into the bag and slipstitch in place just below the holes.

Equipment and Materials

This section describes the general equipment and materials used in the creation of the projects in this book. The list of suppliers on page 118 gives information on where to find the items I used.

Needles

You will need a variety of different needles for the projects in this book.

Tapestry needles These are blunt so they pass through canvas or evenweave without catching. The size required will vary according to the number of strands that you are using and the fabric gauge. The needle, when threaded, should pass easily through the canvas: you should not have to tug it too much and neither should it just drop through. As you stitch, move the needle along the thread so that the same place is not pulled through with each stitch, to stop it wearing in one place. You will find that as you stitch your thread will become twisted, so drop the needle every now and again and let it hang freely to allow the thread to untwist. Do treat yourself to a gold-plated needle for canvaswork: it will never tarnish and will remain beautifully smooth so will always be a pleasure to use.
Crewel needle Use a fine crewel needle with a sharp tip for general hand sewing and when making up the bags.
Beading needle These are very fine, long needles which will be needed for attaching beads, particularly small seed beads.
Knitting needles You will need these for two of the bags. The Venetian Knitted Pouch uses a circular knitting needle, which is a long flexible needle with a point at both ends used to create a seamless piece of work. You may also need a pair of double-pointed knitting needles.

Embroidery Frames

There are many types of frames available and you should choose the one that you are most comfortable with and which fits your budget. Follow the manufacturer's instructions for mounting the canvas or linen. Never use an embroidery hoop on embroidery fabrics unless you have one that is big enough to contain the entire worked area. Where the fabric, especially canvas, has been stretched tightly between the rings it will become distorted, and if this distortion is then stitched over there will be a shadow in the embroidery, which often remains even after stretching.

Scissors

You will need a pair of sharp shears for cutting fabric and also a small pair of sharp-pointed embroidery scissors for cutting threads.

Sewing Machine

I have used a sewing machine for most of the making up of the projects. Mine is a simple one that sews straight lines and zigzags for finishing edges and this is all you need. Of course all the stitching could be done by hand but will take much longer. I also think it is much more difficult to sew a good straight line by hand.

Magnifiers

Do not struggle with your eyesight: go and have an eye test if you are due one and then buy a magnifier if you are still having difficulty. There are many different types of magnifiers – simple ones that sit on your chest, some that clip on to spectacles and others on a stand with integral lighting. Take the time to find the one that suits you best: take some embroidery to the shop and try the magnifier before you buy it.

Other Equipment

If you are already interested in needlework you will probably have a collection of useful tools and accessories, some essential and some just because you like them! Dressmaking pins will be needed when making up some of the bags – those with coloured glass heads are easiest to find when pins have to be removed. An unpicker will help you correct any stitching mistakes. Some sort of thread storage system is helpful to hold the threads that you are working with, and if you think you might have a go at designing or that you might change some of the colours then colour charts are invaluable (ask at your local craft store). Daylight simulation bulbs are very helpful to detect close pastel shades at night.

Embroidery Fabrics

I have used two types of embroidery fabric for the bags in this book – embroidery canvas and evenweave linen, though there are other fabrics available which you may wish to try.

Embroidery canvas This is available in several gauges or mesh sizes and as mono or duo canvas. Remember, your embroidery should be a pleasure, so don't punish yourself by trying to work too fine a canvas. I prefer to use interlock mono canvas, where the threads along the length are in fact double threads twisted together to hold the cross threads firmly in place. This produces a more stable canvas which is easier to make up.
Evenweave linen This is usually used for counted cross stitch and is available in a wide variety of colours and gauges. When cutting canvas or linen for a project add at least 15cm (6in) so you'll end up with at least 5–7.6cm (2–3in) of bare fabric around the finished piece, to allow for making up.

Fabrics

As you can tell from the projects in this book I love silk. Its lustre gives such depth to the colours. There is an enormous variety of fabrics available these days so my best advice is to get out there and look at them all and choose carefully for each project. I buy fabric simply because I have to have it, and it's never there later when you go back trying to find that piece you saw a while ago. Buy plenty and pile it up on your workroom shelves and enjoy just looking at it until you have a project in mind.

Threads

There is a glorious variety of yarns and threads on the market and all stitchers seem to have their own favourites. If you have just discovered a new and tempting thread, do experiment using the charts in this book – you will be amazed and delighted with the effects you can achieve.

Appletons crewel wool This wool thread is easy to use because it is fine enough for the finest canvas, is available in a large range of colours and each colour is produced in a carefully graded range of shades.
Stranded cotton (floss) This mercerized cotton thread has a lovely sheen especially when all six strands are used on canvas. I have used DMC threads but Anchor also has a wide colour range. If you prefer to use Anchor stranded cotton, ask at your local needlecraft store for an Anchor-DMC conversion chart.
Variegated threads A trip to any of the embroidery shows will reveal a wide range of beautiful variegated threads in amazing colour variations. DMC and Anchor ranges include some really pretty shaded threads – some of which I used for the Tooth Fairy and Elf on page 42. For the Lilac and Pearl Amulet on page 24 I used a gorgeous collection of space-dyed threads from Oliver Twists. These are available in many delicious colours which can change the look of a bag completely.
Metallic threads These are available in a fabulous range of colours from various manufacturers and can add a glamorous sparkle to your work. You could use metallic thread on its own, as I have for the delightful little Tooth Fairy on page 42 or try adding a blending filament to your stranded cotton to produce a more subtle gleam. When stitching with metallic threads it is best to work with shorter lengths – about 46cm (18in) – to avoid excessive wear on the thread.

Knitting Wools

There seems to have been an explosion in the types and colours of wools available today and the shops are full of very exciting ranges, most of which are excellent not just for knitting but also for embroidery. I used a multicoloured wool for the Miser's Purse on page 64 which worked beautifully with the seed beads knitted into the purse. The yarn for the Venetian Knitted Pouch

on page 100 was also chosen to tone with some beautiful glass beads I had found.

Beads

We are simply spoiled for choice today with regards beads – it's so hard not to stockpile packet after packet. But at least all that hoarding means there is plenty of choice when it comes to matching beads with fabrics. Beads can be used to embellish a bag, as with the Bags with Attitude on page 38 or form the body of a bag design, like the Peacock Beaded Purse on page 30. The small glass seed beads used for the African Animal bag on page 48 were chosen to provide a textural contrast to the stranded cottons, while the Denim Rose Phone Bag on page 88 features a more colourful beaded rose motif.

Buttons

As you can see by the bags in this book I adore buttons, especially the lovely 'old-fashioned' but now very fashionable mother-of-pearl types, as seen on the Pearly Queen Bag on page 68. Buttons come in all sorts of shapes, sizes, colours and finishes and can be used not just for fastenings but to add an extra textural dimension to your work. Even plain-coloured plastic buttons can lift a design and add just the right finishing touch, as on the Clarice Cliff Satchel on page 20.

Charms

Bags featuring charms can be such fun, and I think those on the Farmyard Tote on page 72 add an extra something to a bag. Sew charms on with matching thread and take care if your bag needs to be washed and ironed.

Decorative Braids and Trims

Decorative trims are another weakness of mine – who can ever have enough of them? My excuse is that they are so versatile. The Easiest Bag in the World shows two variation bags (on page 9) which use decorative trims very effectively and only the smallest quantities are needed, which means you can splash out on some of the fabulous (though sometimes expensive) trims such as marabou and ostrich or some of the bead- and shell-encrusted braids that add instant glamour to the simplest of bags.

Techniques

The techniques described here were used to stitch and make up the bags in this book. It is a good idea to overlock or zigzag fabric edges to prevent fraying and get a good finish especially as a lot of the bags are made in silk which frays prodigiously. Where I have stated a length of fabric in the requirements rather than dimensions this means that you should purchase that length across the width of the fabric as it comes off the roll in the shop. All the seams I used were 1.25cm (½in) unless otherwise stated. You will always get a better finish if you press the seams open as you go rather than trying to do it all at the end.

Preparing Linen

Cut the fabric to the size you need, allowing extra for making up. The edges are soft and do not catch threads like canvas threads do but the fabric will fray quite badly so either oversew the edges by hand or use the zigzag stitch on your sewing machine to preserve the edges.

To avoid working off the edge of the fabric you will need to work the design from the centre of the fabric piece. To find the centre, fold the piece of linen in four and mark the centre with a loop of coloured thread which you can remove once you have started stitching.

Preparing Canvas

Canvas has rough edges where it is cut and your threads will catch on these as you work. It will roughen your embroidery threads and really annoy you. The very best way to deal with these edges is to bind them with soft bias binding. This seems like a lot of trouble but the canvas will be a pleasure to hold as you work it. If you really can't be bothered to do this then use masking tape folded over the edge, but avoid using this tape on stitched areas as it can leave a sticky residue.

For most of the embroidered pieces it is best to start working right in the centre of the canvas from the centre of the chart. This way there is no danger of running out of canvas and working off the edge because your embroidery is not centred properly. Cut the size that you need, deal with the edges, then fold it in four to find the centre point. Mark this with a faint pencil dot and then you are ready to start stitching.

Stretching a Canvas

It is in the nature of canvaswork to distort as it is worked, particularly when using tent stitch. Even if you have used a frame and you think your embroidery is square you should still stretch and starch it – you will be surprised how much the appearance is improved. Not only will the piece be perfectly square but the tension of the stitching will become more even. If you are tempted to miss out this vital stage between the stitching and the finishing your embroidery will never look as good as it might. I would recommend the following method for any of the larger pieces of canvaswork, especially those that are going to be stitched together (for example the Turkish Tassels bag on page 14).

For stretching a canvas
YOU WILL NEED

A large flat clean board (chipboard is ideal)

A sheet of dressmaker's paper (marked in 1cm squares)

Plenty of clean 2.5cm (1in nails) and a small hammer

Cold water starch (available as wallpaper paste – buy a brand without plasticizer, e.g. Lap)

Masking tape

A hard pencil

A small kitchen palette knife (one with a rubber blade is ideal)

1 Start by covering the board with the sheet of squared paper and secure the paper firmly in place with masking tape all around the edge.

2 Place the embroidery, right side down on top of the squared paper. You will be able to see the squares of the paper through the unstitched margin of the canvas. Begin nailing in one corner about 2in (5cm) away from the embroidery. Hammer the nails in just far enough to hold them firmly in the board. Follow one line of holes in the canvas and nail into every second intersection of a line on the paper. It is important to keep the nails no more than 2cm (¾in) apart or the edge of the design will not be straight. When you have completed the first side, go back to the corner and repeat the nailing procedure for the side at right angles to it.

3 Draw a pencil line on the canvas from the last nail on each side to cross at the corner diagonally opposite to the one that you started from. Lift the canvas and, using the squares, find the position on the paper where the lines cross from the nailed corners – this is where the last corner of the canvas must be stretched to. If your work is badly distorted it will help to dampen the embroidery at this stage. If you find you're really struggling with this then allow steam from your steam iron to blow on to the canvas and it will really soften. Pull out the embroidery, nail this last corner and then finish nailing the last two sides.

4 Mix a small quantity of starch paste to the consistency of soft butter and, using the palette knife, spread it evenly but sparingly over the back of the embroidery. Try not to let the starch go over the edges of the embroidery as it will stick to the paper and spoil the board for future use. Allow the work to dry naturally and completely.

5 Remove all the nails from the board and then turn your embroidery over to reveal a beautifully squared and even piece of work.

Stretching a Small Canvas

If you want to stretch a small piece of canvaswork and it isn't too distorted you can just steam iron it. Cover your ironing board with a layer of clean towel. Lay the embroidery face down on the towel and iron the back of the work with plenty of steam – the steam will soften the canvas and enable you to pull it gently back to shape. Never iron on the right side as you will flatten the stitches and remove the sheen from stranded cottons and silks.

Making Bias Binding

Making your own bias binding is easy and will ensure you can make binding that exactly matches or tones with your project, as I did with the Harlequin Lily on page 58 and the Floral Wedding bag collection on page 52. Follow these basic instructions, cutting the bias strips to the width given in the project instructions. Cut enough 4cm (1½in) wide bias strips to make a length of binding sufficient for your project (Fig 1a). To cut on the true bias, fold the selvedge of the fabric to the straight grain widthwise and cut along the fold. This fold will be a true bias cut and will be stretchy. Join all the strips together with narrow seams on a 45-degree angle (Fig 1b).

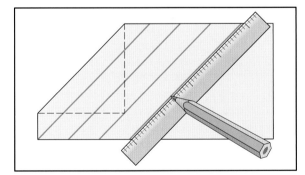

Fig 1a Marking bias strips prior to cutting them

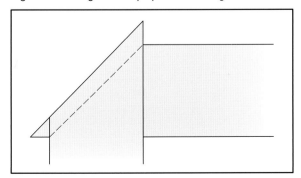

Fig 1b Joining bias strips at a 45-degree angle

Attaching Bias Binding

To attach bias binding, first pin it in place and mark a seam line about 7mm (¼in) from the edge (on ready-made binding this line will already be creased) – see Fig 2a. Sew the binding on by machine, either machining it first on the wrong side and then top stitching down on the right side (Fig 2b) or vice versa if you are nervous about machining a perfectly straight line.

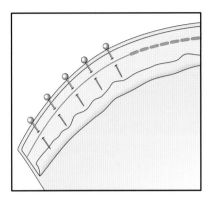

Fig 2a Pinning the binding to the front of the work and machining in place

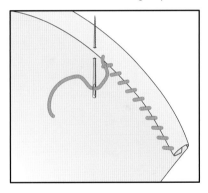

Fig 2b Slipstitching the folded edge to the back of the work

Adding a Zipped Pocket

Several of the bags are open topped and it is a good idea to add a zipped inner pocket to keep a few valuables safe. The easiest way of doing this is to make the pocket the same size as one of the bag sides.

Take one of the pieces of lining, and cut another piece the same width but add on about 8cm (3in) to the length. You will need a zip that is the nearest to the width of this piece that you can buy. Cut about 8cm (3in) from the top of the piece and insert the zip between this top piece and the remaining bottom piece. You may need to adjust the position of the zip in the panel depending on the size of the bag you are making. Now lay the zipped panel on top of the original lining piece and trim the zipped panel to the same size as the lining. Sew them together around the edges and then treat them as one piece of lining. Once the lining is assembled you can open the zip to reveal a pocket between two layers of lining.

Stitches

I have used various stitches in the many bags featured in this book. All of them are easy to work and are described here with the aid of diagrams, many of which show a numbered stitching sequence.

BACKSTITCH

This stitch is used when you want a simple straight line of stitches; this might be to outline a shape or as part of a design.

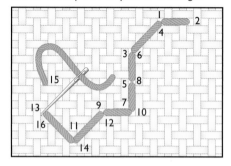

BARGELLO (FLORENTINE STITCH)

Bargello or Florentine embroidery is the name given to designs composed of lomg, straight stitches in distinctive wavy patterns. Work each straight stitch over the number of threads given in the project instructions and in the colours shown on the chart.

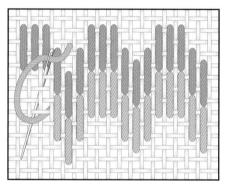

Bargello stitch from the Tassel Purse

BULLION KNOTS

This stitch is very versatile and can be used to create straight or curved bars.

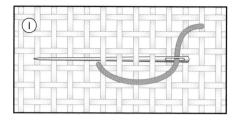

Start with a backstitch exactly where you want the bar to start and finish.

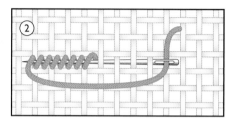

Leave the needle in the fabric and wind a coil on to the needle the same length as the stitch.

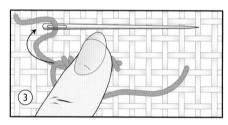

Hold the needle and coil firmly and gently pull the needle through the coil. Flip the bar into place and adjust the coils.

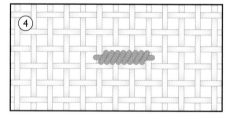

Push the needle through the first hole to the back of the fabric and then finish off, unless you are working another knot.

BUTTONHOLE LOOP

Some purses and bags need a fastening and making a buttonhole loop to fit over a decorative button is an attractive method. To work a buttonhole loop, make two or three stitches to form a loop around the button you are using and then work buttonhole stitches (see below) over the loops to hold them together. Work the stitches tightly together to completely fill the length of the original loops.

Buttonhole loop

BUTTONHOLE STITCH

As well as being used for loops, this stitch can also be worked as a decorative stitch or an edging. Bring your needle up through the fabric on the line where you want a twisted edge. Push it back down through the fabric where the ends of the buttonhole stitch are to be and then up again just next to the first hole, passing it through the loop. Pull the thread gently to make the twisted edge sit well and hold the tension on the thread with your other hand as you make each stitch. You can also make long and short ends to lead into long and short stitch.

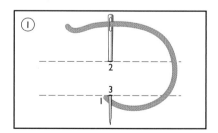

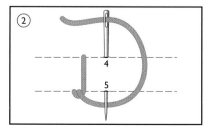

CROSS STITCH

Cross stitch on linen

Cross stitch is the simplest of all counted stitches. When working it on linen (or any evenweave fabric) work over two fabric threads. If you try to work over one thread the stitches will slip under the weave and will not stay in the right place. When working an area of one colour work a row of stitches in one direction first and then complete the cross stitches on the return journey.

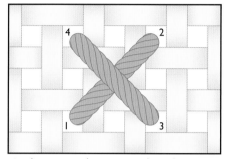

Working a single cross stitch on linen

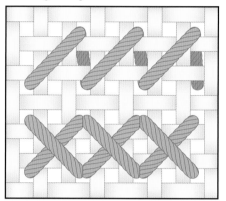

Working cross stitch in two journeys

The tooth fairy bag has cross stitch on linen within a hem-stitched square

Cross stitch on canvas

This is worked in the same way as linen except that when working on interlock canvas you are able to work over one thread as the canvas threads in this type of canvas are locked together. Of course you can still work over two or more threads if you want a large stitch.

FEATHER STITCH

Traditionally, this stitch was always used for crazy patchwork and also on workers' smocks. It is a pretty stitch worked without any counting and gives a very decorative effect. Try to keep the loops of the 'feathers' even.

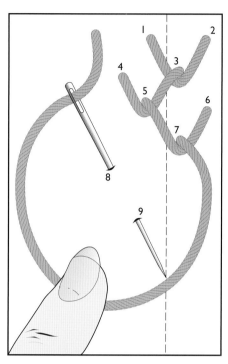

Feather stitch detail from the Crazy Patchwork Handbag

FRENCH KNOTS

These simple little knots can be used to add texture and emphasis. Bring the needle through to the front of the fabric, wind the thread around the needle, post the needle to the back of the fabric one thread away from where you came up, tighten the knot around the base of the needle and take the needle to the back of the fabric. When working in stranded cotton or silk I usually wind the thread twice around the needle but when working with wool I usually only wind once around the needle. This is because wool does not slip well and it is easy for the second turn not to tighten leaving a loopy looking knot. So when working with wool it is better to add extra strands in the needle to make a bigger knot.

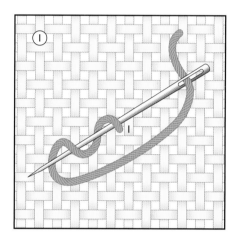

GOBELIN FILLING STITCH

This stitch is used to fill areas of canvaswork. It can be worked over as many canvas threads as you like, can be vertical, horizontal or diagonal and is composed of rows of long stitches that interlink with each other (see picture, below). Take care not to pull the stitches too tightly or you will distort the canvas and the neat appearance of the stitches.

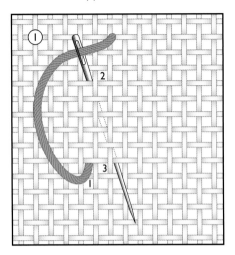

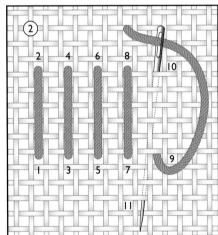

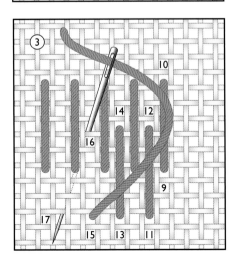

HEM STITCH

Simple hem stitch is really useful on a small project when a turned-over hem would be too bulky. It gives an edge to evenweave fabric that you can cut without the risk of fraying. Work the stitching first and then cut the fabric right up close to the open edge of the hem stitch. If you pull the stitches quite tightly it will make it easier to cut closely, the dashed line on the final diagram shows where to cut.

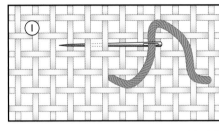

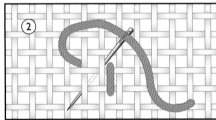

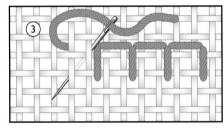

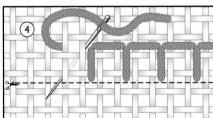

Stitching detail from the Farmyard Tote, showing gobelin filling stitch used on the roof of the farmhouse

LONG-LEGGED CROSS STITCH

Long-legged cross stitch gives a plaited braid effect and is very useful for edging. When worked quite tightly it turns in the edge of canvaswork beautifully and stops the canvas threads showing. When worked over a seam, taking one canvas thread from each edge, it makes an invisible join. The stitch is worked with one short diagonal stitch and then a long one that is twice the length of the short one and crosses it.

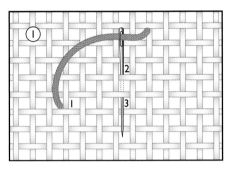

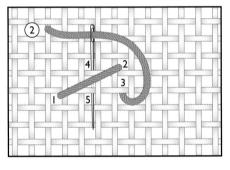

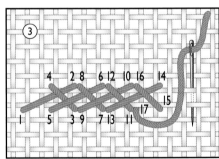

Stitching detail from the Square Amulet purse, showing long-legged cross stitch (at the edges) and areas of satin stitch

LONG AND SHORT STITCH

For this stitch, only the first row worked has long and short stitches, the following rows are all long. Begin at the outside edge and then stitch the following rows into the stitches already worked, splitting the threads to blend the stitches and colours. Don't be afraid to make the stitches longer than you feel you should, as they will be shortened by the next layer of stitching. Do not try to follow the diagrams too rigidly – use them only as a guide because you will have to adapt to the shape that you have to fill.

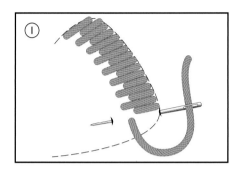

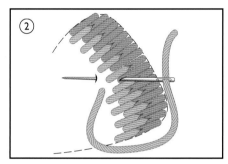

The three-dimensional lily from the Harlequin Lily handbag uses long and short stitch very effectively

RHODES STITCH

Rhodes stitch gives a solid, slightly raised effect, almost like a series of studs on the fabric. It can be worked on evenweave or canvas. Each stitch is worked over a square, usually of four threads by four threads. Work the stitches around the square and as you do so the centre becomes raised. When working a row of Rhodes stitches make sure that you work the same sequence for each stitch for a uniform effect.

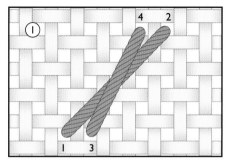

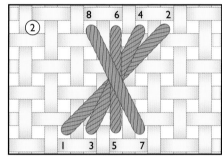

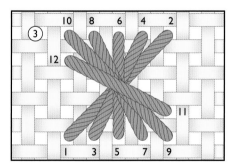

RICE STITCH

Rice stitch is a large cross stitch with an additional stitch worked over each 'leg' of the cross. This additional stitch can be worked in the same colour but when worked in a contrasting shade gives a very pretty effect. Work all the large crosses first and then the contrasting ones. It is usually worked over four threads of either evenweave or canvas.

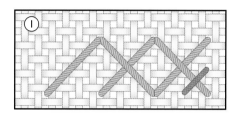

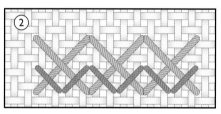

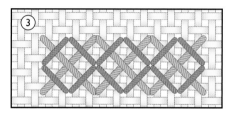

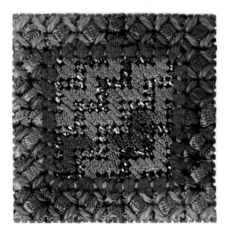

This stitching detail from the Lilac and Pearl Amulet (the variation colourway on page 26) shows rice stitch around the edge and tent stitch zigzags in the centre

SATIN STITCH

Satin stitch is a long smooth stitch used to cover the fabric and fill in regular or irregular shapes. It can be worked diagonally, horizontally or vertically. Lay long stitches next to each other, always bringing your needle up on the same side of the shape so you put as much stitch on the back of the fabric as on the front. The stitch works equally well on evenweave fabric or canvas.

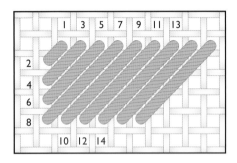

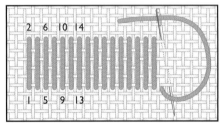

Satin stitch can be worked as squares in alternate directions – in which case it is also called cushion stitch

SPLIT BACKSTITCH

This is similar to ordinary backstitch except that the needle is inserted into the previous stitch. Take care to actually split the thread with your needle. You will find that you can make very smooth curves by making each stitch curve a little as you split it.

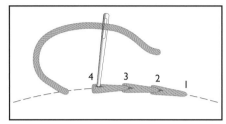

STEM STITCH

This is a simple stitch to work and very useful for free embroidery. Hold the thread down with your finger each time you make a stitch to keep it out of the way and also to maintain an even tension. Try to make your stitches equal in length all along the line but if there is a tight curve to get round it will help to shorten the stitches a little.

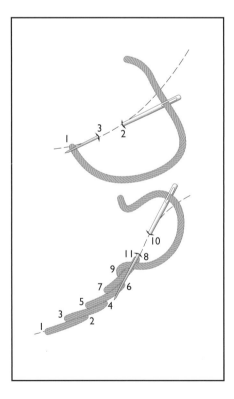

TENT STITCH AND DIAGONAL TENT STITCH

Tent stitch

This should not to be confused with half cross stitch, as it often is. The effect on the front of the work is nearly the same but look at the back to make sure that you are using the right one – tent stitch has long slanting stitches on the back while half cross stitch has little short straight ones. You will obtain a much better effect from tent stitch; the stitches will look fuller and will cover the canvas much better.

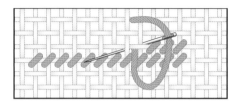

Diagonal tent stitch

This is also known as basketweave because of the woven effect on the reverse. The stitches are worked diagonally across the canvas threads so they distort the canvas less than ordinary tent stitch. This produces an even, full stitch and is pleasing to work. It is a good idea to stitch straight lines of tent stitch for the design and then complete backgrounds in diagonal tent stitch.

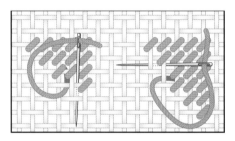

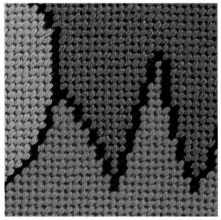

Diagonal tent stitch as used on the Clarice Cliff Satchel

VELVET STITCH

This is basically a cross stitch with an extra loop in it, left long to create a pile on the fabric. The loops can be left as they are or all be cut to the same length. Work velvet stitch in rows from bottom to top and left to right.

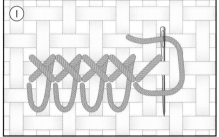

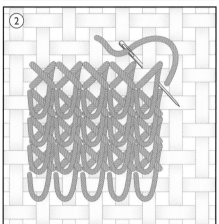

Velvet stitch creates a realistic 'fur' for the Teddy Bear Bag

USING BEADS

Beading on linen

Seed beads are attached with a half cross stitch using fine, strong beading thread and a very fine beading needle. Choose a colour of thread that matches or tones with your background fabric and use the same thread to stitch on all colours of beads. Just occasionally you may need to change a thread colour if you are using really dark or light beads or very transparent ones. Each seed bead occupies the same area as one cross stitch on the same fabric. When buying beads you do need to make sure that you purchase the right size for the fabric that you want to use.

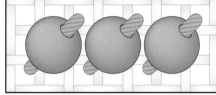

Attaching seed beads

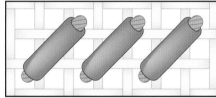

Attaching bugle beads

Beading on canvas

Beading on canvas really works best on double (or Penelope) canvas but this is usually quite hard to find. The double threads support the beads better but when working with single canvas make sure that you keep your stitches tight to stop the beads wobbling around too much because you will be stitching on only one canvas thread. As with beading on linen, you must have the right size of bead.

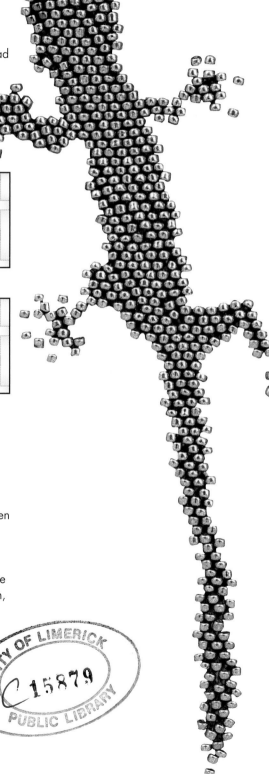

Templates

Where possible templates have been produced actual size for you to trace and use. Some larger patterns have been shown as half a pattern, with a dotted fold line indicating where to double the fabric to create the entire pattern.

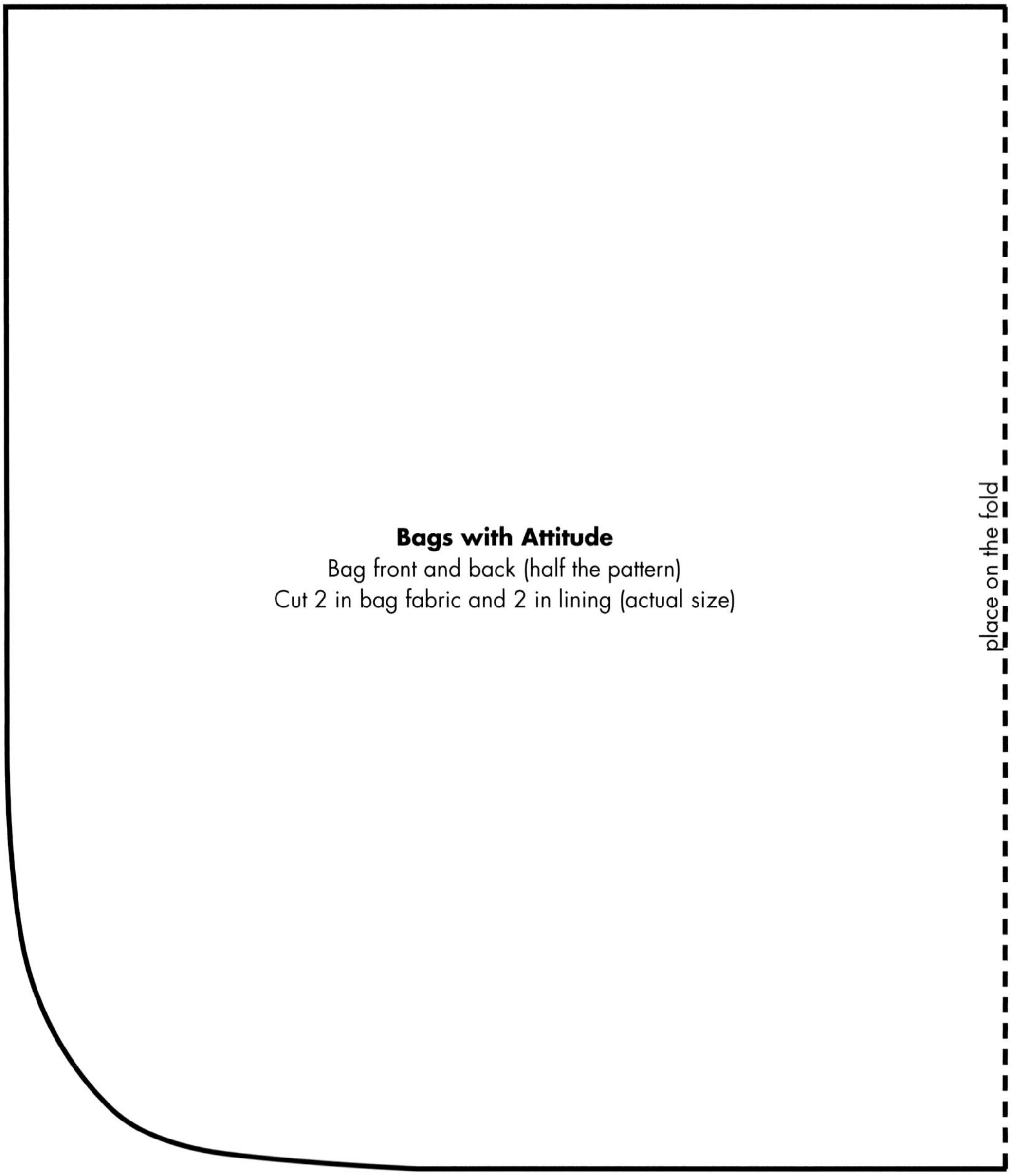

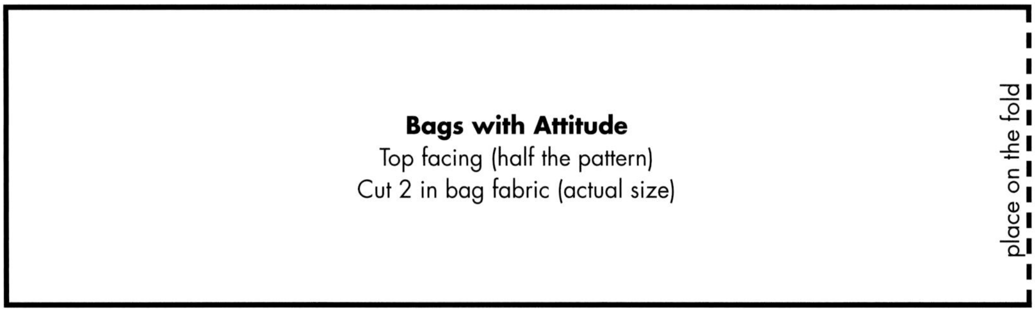

Bags with Attitude
Bag front and back (half the pattern)
Cut 2 in bag fabric and 2 in lining (actual size)

place on the fold

Bags with Attitude
Top facing (half the pattern)
Cut 2 in bag fabric (actual size)

place on the fold

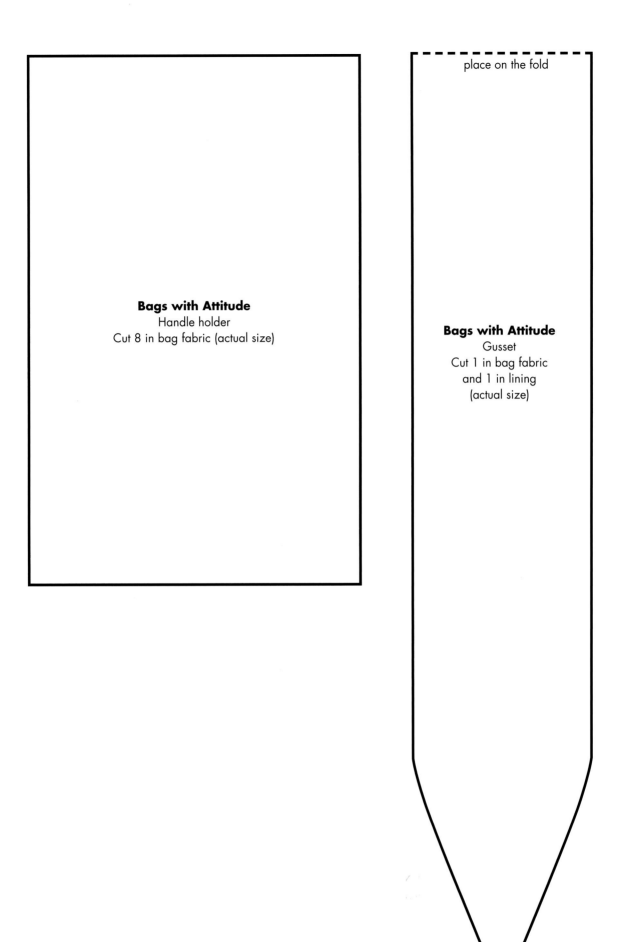

Bags with Attitude
Handle holder
Cut 8 in bag fabric (actual size)

place on the fold

Bags with Attitude
Gusset
Cut 1 in bag fabric
and 1 in lining
(actual size)

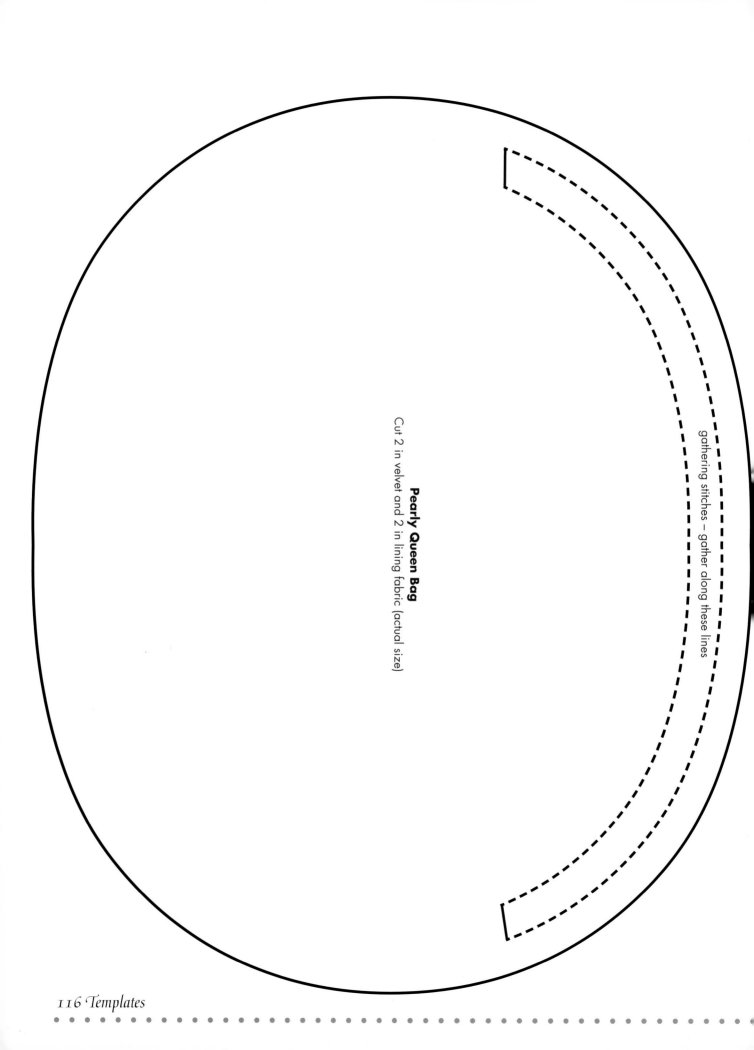

gathering stitches – gather along these lines

Pearly Queen Bag
Cut 2 in velvet and 2 in lining fabric (actual size)

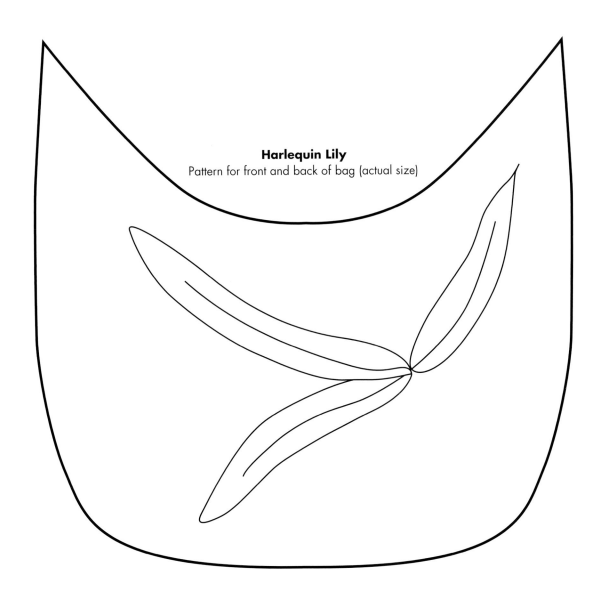

Harlequin Lily
Pattern for front and back of bag (actual size)

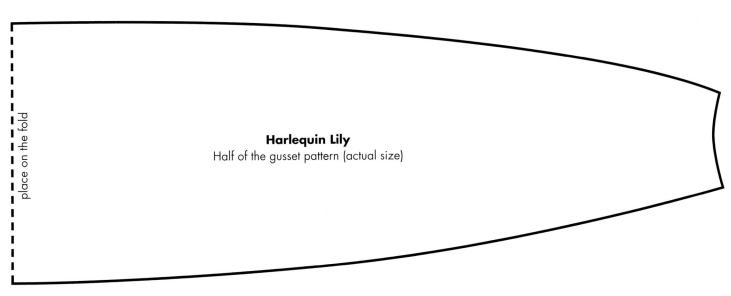

place on the fold

Harlequin Lily
Half of the gusset pattern (actual size)

Suppliers

Coats Crafts UK
PO Box 22, Lingfield Estate, McMullen
Road, Darlington, County Durham
DL1 1YQ
Tel: +44 (0) 1325 365457
(for a list of stockists)
Fax: +44 (0) 1325 338822
*For Anchor stranded cotton (floss) and
other embroidery supplies*

de Haviland Embroidery
Momomark House, 27 Gloucester Street,
London WC1 3XX
Tel: 0207 289 2123

DMC Creative World
Pullman Road, Wigston, Leicestershire
LE18 2DY
Tel: 0116 281 1040
Fax: 0116 281 3592
www.dmc/cw.com
*For stranded cotton (floss) and other
embroidery supplies*

Duttons for Buttons
Oxford Street, Harrogate, Yorkshire
HG1 1QE
Tel: 01423 502092
www.duttonsforbuttons.co.uk
For mother-of-pearl buttons

The John Lewis Partnership
Stores throughout the UK – contact
customer services for one near you
Tel: 08456 049 049
www.johnlewis.com
*For haberdashery, fabrics, knitting wool,
trimmings, buttons, the Venetian glass
beads and Debbie Bliss Maya wool for
the bag on page 100, and much more*

The London Bead Company
339 Kentish Town Road, London
NW5 2TJ
Tel: 0870 2032323
www.londonbeadco.co.uk
*For London Bead Company seed beads
and Mill Hill beads*

Needleworks by Sue Hawkins
East Wing, Highfield House, School Lane,
Whitminster, Gloucestershire GL2 7PJ
*For counted canvaswork, crewelwork and
cross stitch kits as well as upholstered
embroidery frames. For a catalogue
write to the above address or tel 01452
740118.*

Oliver Twists by Jean Oliver
22 Phoenix Road, Crowther, Washington,
Tyne and Wear NE38 0AD
Tel: 0191 416 6016
For 'One Offs' thread collections

Shipston-on-Stour Needlecraft
24/26 Sheep Street, Shipston-on-Stour,
Warwickshire CV36 4AF
Tel: 01608 661616
www.needlecraft.co.uk
*For embroidery supplies of all
descriptions, including Thread Gatherer
Silken Pearl for the Miser's Purse and
charms on the Farmyard Tote (from
the Mary Jane Collection): frog 1140,
ladybird 1104, beehive 1132, bee 1173,
worm 1128, butterfly 1107, blackbird
1106, bluebird 1108, cat 1141*

The Silk Route
Cross Cottage, Cross Lane, Frimley Green,
Surrey GU16 6LN
Tel: 01252 835781
www.thesilkroute.co.uk
*For themed mixed colour packs of
silk dupion*

Stef Francis
Waverley, Higher Roscombe,
Stokeinteignhead, Newton Abbot, Devon
TQ12 4QL
Tel: 01803 323004
www.stef-francis.co.uk
*For Stef Francis space-dyed threads and
fabrics (she will supply a fat quarter of
hand-dyed silk for the Pearly Queen bag)*

The Viking Loom
22 High Petergate, York YO1 7EH
Tel: 01904 765599
www.vikingloom.co.uk
*For the Peacock Purse bag top (Style G90)
and Pearly Queen bag top (Style LSSG 91)*

**Kreinik Manufacturing Company,
Inc**
3106 Timanus Lane, Suite 101, Baltimore,
MD 21244
Tel: 1800 537 2166
Email: kreinik@kreinik.com
www.kreinik.com
*For a wide range of metallic threads
and blending filaments*

MCG Textiles
13845 Magnolia Avenue, Chino,
CA 91710
Tel: 909 591-6351
www.mcgtextiles.com
For embroidery fabrics

**Mill Hill, a division of Wichelt
Imports Inc.**
N162 Hwy 35, Stoddard WI 54658
Tel: 608 788 4600
Fax: 608 788 6040
Email: millhill@millhill.com
www. millhill.com
For Mill Hill beads

M & J Buttons
1000 Sixth Avenue, New York,
NY 10018
Tel: 212 391 6200
www.mjtrim.com
For beads, buttons, ribbons and trimmings

Yarn Tree Designs
PO Box 724, Ames, Iowa 500100724
Tel: 1 800 247 3952
www.yarntree.com
For cross stitch supplies

Zweigart/Joan Toggit Ltd
262 Old New Brunswick Road, Suite E,
Piscataway, NJ 08854-3756
Tel: 732 562 8888
email: info@zweigart.com
www.zweigart.com
For embroidery fabrics

Acknowledgments

My thanks are due to John, Hannah and Jo for putting up with me even when the broomstick comes out! To Vivienne Wells for commissioning the book as well as being a very good friend and to Lin Clements for finding all the mistakes and making me feel as though they weren't my fault. To Ethan Danielson for turning my scribbles into lovely charts and stitch diagrams. To the Inglestone Collection who manufacture and distribute my embroidery kits so well and particularly to Helen Beecroft who pours oil on the waters. To Jane and Bill Greenoff for being understanding about the lack of output to the Cross Stitch Guild while I was working on these bags. And (as always) last, but definitely not least, to my two spaniels Billy and Tommy, who keep me company with their snoring while I work, hear everything but divulge nothing, take me out for walks and make me laugh.

About the Author

Sue Hawkins began her career working for an antique dealer, restoring 17th-century English embroidery. Her knowledge of the needlework business was gained while owning and running an embroidery shop for several years, and since 1991 she has run her own successful kit-manufacturing company, Needleworks (see Suppliers). Sue also teaches embroidery workshops at her home and around the country. Many of her workshops are run on behalf of the Cross Stitch Guild, of which she is technical director. This is Sue's seventh book for David & Charles, her last three being *Dolls House DIY: Carpets and Rugs*, *Dolls House DIY: Embroidered Projects* and *Crewel Embroidery*. Sue lives near Stroud, Gloucestershire, UK.

Index